CONTENTS

INTRODUCTION

For many of us, the subtle aroma of baking bread stirs childhood memories of our grandma's kitchen. And, for the true bread-lover, nothing is more satisfying than catching a whiff of warm bread and enjoying that first fresh, hot slice. Whether it's old-fashioned white or your favorite whole grain, the smell and taste of freshly baked bread are irresistible.

With Better Homes and Gardens® *More Bread Machine Bounty* and your bread machine, making bread at home is simpler, easier, and quicker than ever before. Even the busiest people can enjoy this pleasure daily. In *More Bread Machine Bounty* you'll find more than 100 enticing recipes developed to work in any bread machine. Best of all, you can try these tempting recipes with the confidence that each one has been carefully tested for quality in our Better Homes and Gardens® Test Kitchen. Enjoy!

Bread Machine Basics

If you've just purchased your bread machine, this section will provide you with tips on ingredients and using the machine. Experienced bread machine bakers will also want to review this section for information specific to the recipes in this book.

Recipe Testing

Every recipe in this book was tested by one of ten experienced home economists in the Better Homes and Gardens® Test Kitchen. Recipes were judged on ease of preparation, texture, appeal, and flavor. No recipe can receive the Test Kitchen Seal of Approval until it meets the Test Kitchen's high standards.

Most bread machines have the capacity to make either a 1-pound or 1-1/2-pound loaf, although some only make the smaller size. Most recipes list ingredients in two different amounts so you may simply select which is appropriate for your machine or for your needs. To ensure success in many different machines, recipes in this book were tested in machines from a variety of manufacturers including Chefmate, Hitachi, Maxim, Regal, Panasonic/National, Sanyo, Welbilt, and Zojirushi.

Many recipes in this book call for 1 teaspoon of active dry yeast; note that more yeast is often called for in recipes supplied by bread machine manufacturers. Since one package of yeast (2-1/2 teaspoons) is enough to make two loaves of bread conventionally and our recipes make one loaf in the bread machine, 1 teaspoon of yeast is sufficient for either a 1- or 1-1/2-pound recipe. If you like, you may add additional yeast to our recipes to create a loaf of bread consistent with your taste preferences.

Some Tips from our Test Kitchen

■ It's important to read your manufacturer's directions and add the ingredients to the machine in the order recommended.

■ Since machines vary, it is important to check the dough after the first 3 to 5 minutes of kneading. If the dough looks dry and crumbly, or forms two or more balls, add liquid, 1 tablespoon at a time, until one smooth ball of dough is obtained. If the dough has too much moisture and is unable to form into a ball, add 1 tablespoon of bread flour at a time until a ball does form.

■ All ingredients should be brought to room temperature before they are added to the machine. This includes any ingredients that are cooked or stored in the refrigerator. (Do not leave eggs at room temperature for more than 30 minutes.)

■ You can quickly bring about 1 cup of cold milk to room temperature by microwaving it on 100% (high) power for about 1 minute; stir to evenly distribute the heat.

■ When using margarine or butter, cut it into small pieces to ensure that it is properly blended with the other ingredients.

■ Light colored dried fruits such as apricots and light raisins can inhibit yeast performance because of the preservatives added to the fruit. We do not recommend using these dried fruits in our recipes.

■ Use the end of the handle of a wooden spoon to remove the kneading paddle from the hot loaf of bread.

Measuring Techniques

Correctly and accurately measuring ingredients is important for successful bread baking. But not all ingredients are measured the same way. Here are some guidelines for specific ingredients.

■ **Liquids:** Use a glass or clear plastic measuring cup. Place the cup on a level surface and bend down so your eye is level with the marking you wish to read. Fill the cup to the marking. Don't lift the cup off the counter to your eye; your hand is not as steady as a countertop. When using measuring spoons to measure liquids, pour the liquid just to the top of the spoon without letting it spill over. Avoid measuring over the mixing bowl because the liquid could overflow from the spoon into the bowl.

■ **Flour:** Stir the flour in the canister to lighten. Then gently spoon the flour into a dry measuring cup and level off the top with the straight edge of a knife or metal spatula.

■ **Sugar:** Press brown sugar firmly into a dry measuring cup so that it holds the shape of the cup when turned out. To measure granulated sugar, spoon the sugar into a dry measuring cup, then level it off with the straight edge of a knife or metal spatula.

■ **Shortening:** Using a rubber spatula, press the shortening firmly into a dry measuring cup. Level it off with the straight edge of a knife or a metal spatula.

■ **Margarine or Butter:** For margarine or butter in premeasured sticks, use a sharp knife to cut off the amount needed, following the guidelines on the wrapper. (Use one 1/4-pound stick for 1/2 cup, or half of a stick for 1/4 cup.) For margarine or butter not in premeasured sticks, soften it and measure as directed for solid shortening.

Substitutions

■ Refrigerated or frozen egg substitutes may be used in place of whole eggs (1 egg equals 1/4 cup egg substitute). Egg whites can also be used instead of whole eggs.

■ Sour milk or low-fat plain yogurt are good substitutes for buttermilk. To make sour milk, add 1 tablespoon of vinegar or lemon juice to a 1-cup liquid measuring cup, then add lowfat milk to equal 1 cup.

■ Use the following chart as a reference when you want to use powdered milk instead of regular milk. For example, if the recipe calls for 1/2 cup milk, use 2 tablespoons dry milk powder plus 1/2 cup water.

Regular milk	Dry milk powder	Water
1/2 cup	2 tablespoons	1/2 cup
2/3 cup	2 tablespoons	2/3 cup
3/4 cup	3 tablespoons	3/4 cup
1 cup	1/4 cup	1 cup
1-1/4 cups	1/3 cup	1-1/4 cups
1-1/3 cups	1/3 cup + 1 tablespoon	1-1/4 cups
1-1/2 cups	1/2 cup	1-1/3 cups

Storing Bread Dough and Baked Bread

■ **To freeze bread dough**, place the bread in an airtight container and seal, label, and freeze for up to 3 months. To use the dough, let it stand about 3 hours at room temperature or until thawed. Or, thaw it overnight in the refrigerator. For short term storage, you can refrigerate bread dough for up to 24 hours in an airtight container. Bring the bread to room temperature before shaping it.

■ **To store baked bread**, cool the bread completely; for several hours. (Be sure to remove the bread from the machine immediately after it is baked; proper cooling will prevent it from turning damp and soggy on the outside.) Wrap the cooled bread in foil or plastic wrap, or place it in a plastic bag. Store it in a cool, dry place for up to 3 days. To freeze, place the bread in a freezer bag or container, or tightly wrap it in heavy foil. Freeze for up to 3 months. To serve, thaw the bread in the package for 1 hour, or wrap it in foil and place in a 300° oven for about 20 minutes.

Basic Ingredient Glossary

■ **Amaranth flour** is made from a high-protein, off white grain the size of poppy seeds.* Amaranth has a nutty taste and contains more protein and fiber than corn, rice, or wheat. The grain is usually combined with other grains or flours because of its assertive flavor and heavy texture.

■ **Bread flour**, made from hard wheat, has a higher protein and gluten content than all-purpose flour. Gluten provides structure and height to breads, making bread flour well-suited for use in breads. Bread flour is a form of wheat flour.*

■ **Buckwheat flour** is made from whole, unpolished, unroasted buckwheat kernels.* Light buckwheat flour has very little hull. Dark buckwheat flour has more hull and a stronger flavor. It has a definite earthy and tart flavor and gives a grayish color to the finished product.

■ **Gluten flour** or wheat gluten is made by removing most of the starch from high-protein, hard wheat flour, leaving a product high in gluten.* All flour contains some gluten which is an elastic protein. Adding gluten flour to breads, especially those made with low-gluten flours, improves the texture of the loaf.

■ **Rye flour** is finely ground from rye, a cereal grain with dark brown kernels and a distinctive, robust flavor. Light rye flour is sifted (also called bolted) and contains less bran than dark rye flour.*

■ **Whole wheat flour** is unlike wheat flour or white flour; it is ground from the complete wheat berry and contains the wheat germ as well as the wheat bran.* It is coarser in texture and does not rise as well as regular flour.

■ **Salt** is necessary when making yeast bread. It controls the growth of the yeast which helps the rising of the dough.

■ **Yeast** feeds on the sugar in the dough, producing carbon dioxide gas that makes the dough rise. Active dry yeast is simply dried granules of yeast. Yeast amounts used in bread machine recipes vary considerably among manufacturers due to the many factors contributing to yeast performance. When baking bread at high altitudes, it may be necessary to reduce the amount of yeast in any given bread recipe. Refer to your bread machine manufacturer's directions regarding high altitude baking.

*Flours and grains may be stored in an airtight container at room temperature for up to 5 months. For longer storage, keep in the refrigerator or freezer.

Machine Settings and Cycles

Machines vary with different cycles, baking times, and temperatures. Here are several common cycles to compare with your owner's manual.

■ **Basic white:** This is the all-purpose setting for any machine. Most breads (except one high in whole grains) should work on this cycle.

■ **Sweet:** Use the sweet cycle when available for breads high in sugar. Some sweet cycles may have different rising times while others have a different baking temperature to compensate for higher amounts of sugar in a bread dough. Sweet cycle is similar to the basic white cycle.

■ **Whole grain:** All machines are capable of handling whole grain or rye breads. Whole grain cycles usually are geared to longer rising times for these heavier breads.

■ **Raisin:** Some machines have a separate cycle with a beep about 5 minutes prior to the end of the second kneading cycle. This beep indicates that raisins, nuts, or similar ingredients can be added at that time. If your machine has no beep, try adding additional ingredients 25 minutes into the cycle.

■ **Dough:** This cycle mixes and kneads the bread dough, then allows it to rise once before the cyle is complete. At this point, you can shape and bake the bread conventionally. If your machine's dough cycle does not allow for one rising, place the dough in a greased bowl. Cover and let rise in a warm place for about 1 hour or till nearly double. Continue as directed in recipe.

■ **Crust Color Setting:** The best choice for most breads is the medium setting. Recipes high in sugar may be baked using a lighter setting, if available.

■ **Timer:** Recipes using milk, eggs, cheese, or other foods which may spoil sitting at room temperature for long periods of time should not be used with the timer. Dry milk powder and water should be substituted for regular milk when making bread with the timer (see chart, page 10).

Nutrition Calculations

You can keep track of your daily nutrition needs by using the nutrition analysis provided at the end of each recipe. For this book, the calculations are for one serving of the 1-pound loaf. (Each 1-pound loaf makes 16 servings unless noted otherwise.) When a recipe gives an ingredient substitution, the first choice is used in the nutrition analysis. Optional ingredients are not included.

CLASSIC BREADS

ALL-AMERICAN WHITE BREAD

1 Pound	Ingredients	1-1/2 Pound
3/4 cup	milk	1-1/4 cups
1 tablespoon	margarine *or* butter	4 teaspoons
2 cups	bread flour	3 cups
1 tablespoon	sugar	4 teaspoons
1/2 teaspoon	salt	3/4 teaspoon
1 teaspoon	active dry yeast	1 teaspoon

Select loaf size. Add ingredients to machine according to manufacturer's directions.

Canola White Bread: Prepare as directed above, except substitute canola oil for the margarine, using 2 teaspoons for the 1-pound loaf or 1 tablespoon for the 1-1/2-pound loaf.

Fructose White Bread: Prepare as directed above, except substitute fructose for the sugar, using 1 teaspoon for the 1-pound loaf or 1-1/2 teaspoons for the 1-1/2 pound loaf.

Per serving: 77calories, 2 g protein, 14 g carbohydrate, 1 g total fat (0 g saturated), 1 mg cholesterol, 81 mg sodium, 38 mg potassium.

BLUE CHEESE BREAD

1 Pound	Ingredients	1-1/2 Pound
2/3 cup	water	1 cup
1 tablespoon	margarine *or* butter, softened	4 teaspoons
1/3 cup	blue cheese, crumbled	1/2 cup
1/4 cup	grated Parmesan cheese	1/3 cup
2 cups	bread flour	3 cups
1 tablespoon	sugar	4 teaspoons
1/2 teaspoon	onion salt	3/4 teaspoon
1 teaspoon	active dry yeast	1 teaspoon

Select loaf size. Add ingredients to machine according to manufacturer's directions. Use the light setting, if available.

Per serving: 89 calories, 3 g protein, 13 g carbohydrate, 2 g total fat (1 g saturated), 3 mg cholesterol, 77 mg sodium, 30 mg potassium.

CHEESY POPPY SEED BREAD

1 Pound	Ingredients	1-1/2 Pound
2/3 cup	milk	1 cup
1	egg	1
1/2 cup (2 ounces)	shredded Swiss cheese	3/4 cup (3 ounces)
2 tablespoons	margarine *or* butter	3 tablespoons
2 cups	bread flour	3 cups
1 teaspoon	sugar	2 teaspoons
1 tablespoon	poppy seed	4 teaspoons
1/2 teaspoon	salt	3/4 teaspoon
1/2 teaspoon	finely shredded lemon peel	3/4 teaspoon
1 teaspoon	active dry yeast	1 teaspoon

Select loaf size. Add ingredients to machine according to manufacturer's directions.

Per serving: 94 calories, 4 g protein, 13 g carbohydrate, 3 g total fat (0 g saturated), 3 mg cholesterol, 104 mg sodium, 40 mg potassium.

CHEDDAR-BUTTERMILK BREAD

1 Pound	Ingredients	1-1/2 Pound
3/4 cup	buttermilk	1-1/4 cups
1	egg	1
1/2 cup (2 ounces)	shredded sharp cheddar cheese	3/4 cup (3 ounces)
2 cups	bread flour	3 cups
2 teaspoons	sugar	1 tablespoon
1/2 teaspoon	salt	3/4 teaspoon
1 teaspoon	active dry yeast	1 teaspoon

Select loaf size. Add ingredients to machine according to manufacturer's directions. Use the light setting, if available.

Per serving: 88 calories, 4 g protein, 14 g carbohydrate, 2 g total fat (1 g saturated), 17 mg cholesterol, 105 mg sodium, 45 mg potassium.

CHEESY POTATO BREAD

1 Pound	Ingredients	1-1/2 Pound
1/2 cup	water	3/4 cup
1/3 cup	chopped, peeled potato	1/2 cup
1/3 cup	milk	1/2 cup
1/4 cup	shredded cheddar cheese	1/3 cup
1-1/2 teaspoons	margarine *or* butter	2 teaspoons
2-1/4 cups	bread flour	3-1/3 cups
2 teaspoons	sugar	1 tablespoon
1/2 teaspoon	onion salt	3/4 teaspoon
1/4 teaspoon	caraway seed, crushed	1/4 teaspoon
1 teaspoon	active dry yeast	1 teaspoon

Select loaf size. In a small saucepan combine water and potato. Bring to boiling; reduce heat. Cover and simmer about 10 minutes or till potato is very tender. Do not drain. Mash potato in the water. Measure 1/2 cup potato-water mixture. If necessary, add water to equal 1/2 cup for 1-pound loaf (2/3 cup for 1-1/2-pound loaf); discard excess. Cool.

Add potato mixture and remaining ingredients to machine according to manufacturer's directions.

Per serving: 87 calories, 3 g protein, 16 g carbohydrate, 1 g total fat (0 g saturated), 1 mg cholesterol, 119 mg sodium, 58 mg potassium.

ALL-AMERICAN BEER BREAD

1 Pound	Ingredients	1-1/2 Pound
3/4 cup	dark beer *or* beer	1 cup + 2 tablespoons
2 teaspoons	margarine *or* butter	1 tablespoon
1-1/3 cups	whole wheat flour	2-1/4 cups
2/3 cup	bread flour	1 cup
1 tablespoon	honey *or* molasses	2 tablespoons
1/2 teaspoon	salt	3/4 teaspoon
1 teaspoon	active dry yeast	1 teaspoon

Select loaf size. Add ingredients to machine according to manufacturer's directions.

Per serving: 72 calories, 2 g protein, 14 g carbohydrate, 1 g total fat (0 g saturated), 0 mg cholesterol, 73 mg sodium, 56 mg potassium.

Champagne Bread

1 Pound	Ingredients	1-1/2 Pound
2/3 cup	brut champagne*	1 cup
1 teaspoon	active dry yeast	1 teaspoon
2/3 cup	bread flour	1 cup
1	egg	1
1 tablespoon	margarine *or* butter	2 tablespoons
1 cup + 2 tablespoons	bread flour	1-3/4 cups
2 tablespoons	instant nonfat dry milk powder	3 tablespoons
1 teaspoon	sugar	1-1/2 teaspoons
1/2 teaspoon	salt	3/4 teaspoon
1 teaspoon	active dry yeast	1 teaspoon

For the sponge (the starter): Select loaf size. Pour champagne into a medium mixing bowl. Sprinkle 1 teaspoon yeast over champagne; stir to dissolve. Add the flour, using 2/3 cup for the 1-pound loaf or 1 cup for the 1-1/2-pound loaf. Mix well. Cover with plastic wrap; set in a warm place (room temperature) for at least 12 hours.

To finish the bread: Add sponge and remaining ingredients to machine according to manufacturer's directions.

*Note: This elegant white loaf requires brut champagne which is dry. It is necessary to start this recipe the night before because the sponge (or the starter) must sit in a warm place for 12 hours.

Per serving: 76 calories, 3 g protein, 12 g carbohydrate, 1 g total fat (0 g saturated), 13 mg cholesterol, 82 mg sodium, 35 mg potassium.

Basic Egg Bread

1 Pound	Ingredients	1-1/2 Pound
2/3 cup	milk	1 cup
1	egg	1
2 teaspoons	margarine *or* butter	1 tablespoon
2 cups	bread flour	3 cups
4 teaspoons	sugar	2 tablespoons
1/2 teaspoon	salt	3/4 teaspoon
1 teaspoon	active dry yeast	1 teaspoon

Select loaf size. Add ingredients to machine according to manufacturer's directions.

Per serving: 80 calories, 3 g protein, 14 g carbohydrate, 1 g total fat (0 g saturated), 14 mg cholesterol, 75 mg sodium, 40 mg potassium.

Hawaiian-Style Bread

1 Pound	Ingredients	1-1/2 Pound
2/3 cup	buttermilk	1 cup
1	egg	1
1-1/2 teaspoons	margarine *or* butter	1 tablespoon
2 cups	bread flour	3 cups
1/4 cup	whole wheat flour	1/3 cup
2 teaspoons	sugar	1 tablespoon
1/2 teaspoon	salt	3/4 teaspoon
1 teaspoon	active dry yeast	1 teaspoon
1/4 cup	coarsely chopped macadamia nuts *or* sliced almonds	1/3 cup
1/3 cup	coconut, toasted	1/2 cup
1/3 cup	chopped dried *or* candied pineapple	1/2 cup
1 recipe	Vanilla Icing (optional)	1 recipe

Select loaf size. Add ingredients to machine according to manufacturer's directions. If desired, before serving, glaze with Vanilla Icing; sprinkle with additional candied fruit and nuts.

Vanilla Icing: In a small mixing bowl stir together 1 cup sifted *powdered sugar*, 1/4 teaspoon *vanilla*, and enough *milk* (2 to 3 teaspoons) to make an icing of drizzling consistency. Makes 1/2 cup.

Per serving: 117 calories, 3 g protein, 19 g carbohydrate, 3 g total fat (1 g saturated), 14 mg cholesterol, 91 mg sodium, 93 mg potassium.

OLD-FASHIONED MAPLE BREAD

1 Pound	Ingredients	1-1/2 Pound
3/4 cup	milk	1 cup + 2 tablespoons
1/2 teaspoon	maple flavoring	3/4 teaspoon
2 cups	bread flour	3 cups
4 teaspoons	brown sugar	2 tablespoons
1/2 teaspoon	salt	3/4 teaspoon
1 teaspoon	active dry yeast	1 teaspoon

Select loaf size. Add ingredients to machine according to manufacturer's directions.

Per serving: 81 calories, 2 g protein, 14 g carbohydrate, 1 g total fat (0 g saturated), 1 mg cholesterol, 84 mg sodium, 42 mg potassium.

SOURDOUGH BREADS

Basic Sourdough Starter

Ingredients

1 package active dry yeast

1/2 cup warm water (105° to 115°)

2 cups warm water (105° to 115°)

2 cups all-purpose flour

1 tablespoon sugar *or* honey

In a large mixing bowl dissolve yeast in 1/2 cup warm water. Stir in 2 cups warm water, flour, and sugar or honey. Beat with an electric mixer on medium speed till smooth.

Cover bowl with 100% cotton cheesecloth. Let the mixture stand at room temperature for 5 to 10 days, or till it has a fermented aroma, stirring it 2 to 3 times a day. (The warmer the room, the faster the fermentation.)

To store the starter, transfer to a jar, cover with 100% cotton cheesecloth, and refrigerate till ready to use. Do not cover tightly or use a metal lid.

To use starter, bring desired amount to room temperature. For each cup of starter used, replenish remaining starter by adding 3/4 cup all-purpose flour, 3/4 cup water, and 1 teaspoon sugar or honey. Cover and let mixture stand at room temperature for at least 1 day or till it is bubbly. Refrigerate starter for later use.

If you have not used the starter within 10 days, stir in 1 teaspoon of sugar or honey. Repeat every 10 days unless starter is replenished.

Note: Starter should be the consistency of thin pancake batter. Add water, if necessary, before using.

BASIC SAN FRANCISCO-STYLE BREAD

1 Pound	Ingredients	1-1/2 Pound
3/4 cup	Basic Sourdough Starter (page 28)	1-1/4 cups
1/4 cup	milk	2 tablespoons
2 cups	bread flour	3 cups
2 teaspoons	sugar	1 tablespoon
1/2 teaspoon	salt	3/4 teaspoon
1 teaspoon	active dry yeast	1 teaspoon
	cornmeal	

Select loaf size. Add all ingredients, except cornmeal, to machine according to manu-facturer's directions for the dough cycle. After completing the dough cycle, remove the dough from the machine. Cover and let rest for 10 minutes.

Lightly grease a baking sheet; sprinkle with cornmeal. Set aside. On a lightly floured surface, shape dough into one 6-inch round for 1-pound loaf or one 8-inch round for 1-1/2-pound loaf. (Or, roll 1-pound dough into a 14x9-inch rectangle or divide 1-1/2-pound dough in half and roll each half into a 9x7-inch rectangle.)

Starting from one of the long sides, roll up jelly-roll style; seal well. Pinch and pull ends to taper. Place rolls, seam side down, on prepared baking sheet. Using a sharp knife, slash top of bread diagonally. Cover and let rise in a warm place for 30 to 45 minutes or till nearly double.

Brush top with water. Bake in a 400° oven for 20 to 30 minutes or till crust is golden brown and bread sounds hollow when tapped. Remove from oven; cool on a wire rack.

Per serving: 91 calories, 3 g protein, 18 g carbohydrate, 0 g total fat (0 g saturated), 0 mg cholesterol, 69 mg sodium, 37 mg potassium.

SOURDOUGH CHEESE BREAD

1 Pound	Ingredients	1-1/2 Pound
3/4 cup	Basic Sourdough Starter (page 28)	1-1/4 cups
1/3 cup	milk	1/3 cup
2 ounces	cream cheese, softened	3 ounces
1 tablespoon	cooking oil	1 tablespoon
1-1/2 cups	bread flour	2-1/4 cups
1 cup	rye flour	1-1/2 cups
1 tablespoon	gluten flour	2 tablespoons
2 teaspoons	honey	1 tablespoon
3 tablespoons	snipped fresh chives	1/4 cup
1/2 teaspoon	salt	3/4 teaspoon
1/2 teaspoon	caraway seed	1 teaspoon
1 teaspoon	active dry yeast	1 teaspoon

Select loaf size. Add ingredients to machine according to manufacturer's directions.

Per serving: 121 calories, 4 g protein, 21 g carbohydrate, 3 g total fat (1 g saturated), 4 mg cholesterol, 81 mg sodium, 56 mg potassium.

Cornmeal Sourdough Bread

1 Pound	Ingredients	1-1/2 Pound
3/4 cup	Basic Sourdough Starter (page 28)	1-1/4 cups
1/4 cup	low-fat milk	1/4 cup
2 teaspoons	margarine *or* butter	1 tablespoon
1-3/4 cups	bread flour	2-2/3 cups
1/3 cup	cornmeal	1/3 cup
1 tablespoon	honey	2 tablespoons
3/4 teaspoon	salt	1 teaspoon
1 small	jalapeño pepper, finely chopped (optional)	1 large
1 teaspoon	active dry yeast	1 teaspoon

Select loaf size. Add ingredients to machine according to manufacturer's directions.

Per serving: 98 calories, 3 g protein, 19 g carbohydrate, 1 g total fat (0 g saturated), 0 mg cholesterol, 115 mg sodium, 41 mg potassium.

Sourdough Wheat Bread

1 Pound	Ingredients	1-1/2 Pound
3/4 cup	Basic Sourdough Starter (page 28)	1-1/4 cups
1/4 cup	milk	1/3 cup
1 tablespoon	margarine *or* butter	1 tablespoon
1-1/4 cups	bread flour	1-3/4 cups
1 cup	whole wheat flour	1-1/4 cups
1 teaspoon	sugar	2 teaspoons
3/4 teaspoon	salt	1 teaspoon
1 teaspoon	active dry yeast	1 teaspoon

Select loaf size. Add ingredients to machine according to manufacturer's directions.

Per serving: 97 calories, 3 g protein, 19 g carbohydrate, 1 g total fat (0 g saturated), 0 mg cholesterol, 111 mg sodium, 61 mg potassium.

Garlic Sourdough Bread

1 Pound	Ingredients	1-1/2 Pound
3/4 cup	Basic Sourdough Starter (page 28)	1-1/4 cups
1/4 cup	milk	2 tablespoons
1/3 cup	grated Parmesan cheese	1/2 cup
1 tablespoon	cooking oil	1 tablespoon
2 cups	bread flour	3 cups
2 teaspoons	honey	1 tablespoon
1 clove	garlic, minced, *or*	2 cloves
1/8 teaspoon	garlic powder	1/4 teaspoon
1/2 teaspoon	salt	3/4 teaspoon
1 teaspoon	active dry yeast	1 teaspoon

Select loaf size. Add ingredients to machine according to manufacturer's directions.

Per serving: 107 calories, 4 g protein, 18 g carbohydrate, 2 g total fat (1 g saturated), 2 mg cholesterol, 108 mg sodium, 40 mg potassium.

Oatmeal Sourdough Bread

1 Pound	Ingredients	1-1/2 Pound
1/2 cup	Basic Sourdough Starter (page 28)	3/4 cup
1/2 cup	milk	3/4 cup
1 tablespoon	margarine *or* butter	4 teaspoons
2 cups	bread flour	3 cups
1/4 cup	toasted rolled oats*	1/3 cup
2 teaspoons	sugar	1 tablespoon
1/2 teaspoon	salt	3/4 teaspoon
1 teaspoon	active dry yeast	1 teaspoon

Select loaf size. Add ingredients to machine according to manufacturer's directions.

*Note: To toast rolled oats, place oats in a shallow baking pan. Bake in a 350° oven for 15 to 20 minutes or till light brown. Cool.

Per serving: 93 calories, 3 g protein, 17 g carbohydrate, 1 g total fat (0 g saturated), 1 mg cholesterol, 79 mg sodium, 43 mg potassium.

Sourdough Rye Bread

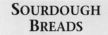

1 Pound	Ingredients	1-1/2 Pound
3/4 teaspoon	active dry yeast	1 teaspoon
1 cup	warm water (105° to 115°)	1-1/2 cups
1/2 cup	rye flour	3/4 cup
1	egg	1
1 tablespoon	olive oil	1 tablespoon
1-1/2 cups	bread flour	2-1/4 cups
1/2 cup	rye flour	3/4 cup
2 tablespoons	gluten flour	3 tablespoons
1 tablespoon	molasses	2 tablespoons
2 teaspoons	caraway seed	1 tablespoon
3/4 teaspoon	salt	1 teaspoon
1 teaspoon	active dry yeast	1 teaspoon

Select loaf size. For the starter, sprinkle yeast over warm water and stir till dissolved; stir in 1/2 cup or 3/4 cup rye flour. Cover bowl with 100% cotton cheesecloth. Let stand at room temperature for 3 days, stirring twice a day. Use the entire starter in the bread recipe.

Add the starter and the remaining ingredients to machine according to manufacturer's directions.

Per serving: 90 calories, 3 g protein, 16 g carbohydrate, 2 g total fat (0 g saturated), 13 mg cholesterol, 106 mg sodium, 79 mg potassium.

Rye Sourdough Starter

Ingredients

1 package active dry yeast
1/2 cup warm water (105° to 115°)
2 cups warm water (105° to 115°)
2 cups rye flour
1 tablespoon sugar *or* honey

In a large mixing bowl dissolve yeast in 1/2 cup warm water. Stir in 2 cups warm water, rye flour, and sugar or honey. Beat with an electric mixer on medium speed till smooth.

Cover bowl with 100% cotton cheesecloth. Let mixture stand at room temperature for 5 to 10 days, or till it has a fermented aroma, stirring it 2 or 3 times a day. (The warmer the room, the faster the fermentation.)

To store, transfer starter to a jar. Cover the jar with 100% cotton cheesecloth and refrigerate. Do not cover the jar tightly or use a metal lid. Use in Pumpernickel Sourdough Bread (page 37) or Whole Wheat Sourdough Bread (page 38).

To use starter, bring desired amount to room temperature. For each cup of starter used, replenish remaining starter by stirring in 3/4 cup rye flour, 3/4 cup water, and 1 teaspoon sugar or honey. Cover and let mixture stand at room temperature at least 1 day or till it is bubbly. Refrigerate starter for later use.

If starter is not used within 10 days, stir in 1 teaspoon sugar or honey. Repeat every 10 days unless starter is replenished.

Note: Starter should be the consistency of thin pancake batter. Add water, if necessary, before using.

PUMPERNICKEL SOURDOUGH BREAD

1 Pound	Ingredients	1-1/2 Pound
3/4 cup	Rye Sourdough Starter (page 36)	1 cup
1/4 cup	cool strong coffee	1/3 cup
1 tablespoon	cooking oil	1 tablespoon
1-1/3 cups	bread flour	2 cups
1/2 cup	rye flour	3/4 cup
1/3 cup	whole wheat flour	1/2 cup
1 tablespoon	gluten flour	2 tablespoons
2 tablespoons	molasses	3 tablespoons
1 tablespoon	unsweetened cocoa powder	4 teaspoons
1 teaspoon	caraway *or* fennel seed	1-1/2 teaspoons
1/2 teaspoon	salt	3/4 teaspoon
1 teaspoon	active dry yeast	1 teaspoon

Select loaf size. Add ingredients to machine according to manufacturer's directions.

Per serving: 93 calories, 3 g protein, 18 g carbohydrate, 1 g total fat (0 g saturated), 0 mg cholesterol, 70 mg sodium, 128 mg potassium.

Whole Wheat Sourdough Bread

1 Pound	Ingredients	1-1/2 Pound
3/4 cup	Rye Sourdough Starter (page 36)	1-1/4 cups
1/4 cup	milk	1/4 cup
1 tablespoon	margarine *or* butter	1 tablespoon
1-1/3 cups	whole wheat flour	2 cups
2/3 cup	bread flour	1 cup
1 tablespoon	brown sugar	2 tablespoons
1/2 teaspoon	salt	3/4 teaspoon
1 teaspoon	active dry yeast	1 teaspoon

Select loaf size. Add ingredients to machine according to manufacturer's directions.

Per serving: 89 calories, 3 g protein, 17 g carbohydrate, 1 g total fat (0 g saturated), 0 mg cholesterol, 78 mg sodium, 68 mg potassium.

WHOLE GRAIN BREADS

Basic Whole Wheat Bread

1 Pound	Ingredients	1-1/2 Pound
3/4 cup + 2 tablespoons	milk	1-1/4 cups
2 teaspoons	margarine *or* butter	1 tablespoon
1-1/3 cups	whole wheat flour	2 cups
2/3 cup	bread flour	1 cup
1 tablespoon	honey *or* sugar	2 tablespoons
1/2 teaspoon	salt	3/4 teaspoon
1 teaspoon	active dry yeast	1 teaspoon

Select loaf size. Add ingredients to machine according to manufacturer's directions.

Add-a-Grain Whole Wheat Bread: If you like, you can add one of the following:
To the 1-pound loaf, choose from 1/2 teaspoon sesame seed, 2 teaspoons wheat bran, 1 tablespoon rolled oats, 2 teaspoons toasted wheat germ, or 1-1/2 teaspoons oat groats. To the 1-1/2-pound loaf, choose from 3/4 teaspoon sesame seed, 1 tablespoon wheat bran, 2 tablespoons rolled oats, 1 tablespoon toasted wheat germ, or 2 teaspoons oat groats.

Per serving: 68 calories, 3 g protein, 13 g carbohydrate, 1 g total fat (0 g saturated), 1 mg cholesterol, 79 mg sodium, 70 mg potassium.

ENGLISH BARLEY BREAD

1 Pound	Ingredients	1-1/2 Pound
2/3 cup	water	1 cup
4 teaspoons	cooking oil	2 tablespoons
1-1/3 cups	bread flour	2 cups
1/3 cup	barley flour	1/2 cup
1/3 cup	whole wheat flour	1/2 cup
2 tablespoons	molasses *or* brown sugar	3 tablespoons
2 tablespoons	nonfat dry milk powder	3 tablespoons
3/4 teaspoon	salt	1 teaspoon
1/2 teaspoon	ground cinnamon	3/4 teaspoon
1 teaspoon	active dry yeast	1 teaspoon

Select loaf size. Add ingredients to machine according to manufacturer's directions.

Per serving: 75 calories, 2 g protein, 14 g carbohydrate, 1 g total fat (0 g saturated), 0 mg cholesterol, 104 mg sodium, 108 mg potassium.

BUTTERMILK WHOLE WHEAT BREAD

1 Pound	Ingredients	1-1/2 Pound
3/4 cup	buttermilk	1-1/3 cups
1	egg	1
2 teaspoons	margarine *or* butter	1 tablespoon
1 cup	bread flour	1-1/2 cups
1 cup	whole wheat flour	1-1/2 cups
1 tablespoon	honey	2 tablespoons
3/4 teaspoon	salt	1 teaspoon
1 teaspoon	active dry yeast	1 teaspoon

Select loaf size. Add ingredients to machine according to manufacturer's directions.

Per serving: 74 calories, 3 g protein, 13 g carbohydrate, 1 g total fat (0 g saturated), 14 mg cholesterol, 122 mg sodium, 64 mg potassium.

CRACKED WHEAT AND HONEY NUT BREAD

1 Pound	Ingredients	1-1/2 Pound
1/4 cup	cracked wheat	1/3 cup
3/4 cup	milk	1-1/4 cups
1 tablespoon	cooking oil	2 tablespoons
1 tablespoon	honey	2 tablespoons
3/4 teaspoon	salt	1 teaspoon
1-1/2 cups	whole wheat flour	2-1/4 cups
3/4 cup	bread flour	1-1/4 cups
1/3 cup	walnuts *or* pecans, chopped	1/2 cup
1 teaspoon	active dry yeast	1 teaspoon

Select loaf size. Bring 1 cup water to boiling. Remove from heat. Add cracked wheat. Soak the cracked wheat for 3 minutes; drain well. Add to milk. Add ingredients to machine according to manufacturer's directions.

Per serving: 114 calories, 4 g protein, 19 g carbohydrate, 3 g total fat (0 g saturated), 1 mg cholesterol, 140 mg sodium, 108 mg potassium.

WHOLE WHEAT FRENCH BREAD

1 Pound	Ingredients	1-1/2 Pound
3/4 cup	water	1 cup + 2 tablespoons
1-1/3 cups	whole wheat flour	2 cups
3/4 cup	bread flour	1-1/4 cups
2 teaspoons	brown sugar	1 tablespoon
1/2 teaspoon	salt	3/4 teaspoon
1 teaspoon	active dry yeast	1 teaspoon
2 teaspoons	cornmeal	1 tablespoon

Select loaf size. Add all ingredients, except cornmeal, according to manufacturer's dough cycle directions. Remove dough from the machine; let rest for 10 minutes.

Grease a baking sheet; sprinkle with cornmeal. On a lightly floured surface, roll 1-pound dough into a 15x10-inch rectangle. (Or, divide the 1-1/2-pound loaf in half; shape into two 10x8-inch rectangles.) Starting at a wide end, roll up the rectangles, jelly-roll style; pinch the ends closed. Place the loaves, seam side down, on prepared baking sheet. Cover and let rise in a warm place for 30 to 35 minutes.

Using a very sharp knife, slash the dough 5 to 6 times (3 to 4 times for smaller loaves). Brush with water. Bake in a 375° oven about 25 minutes or till golden brown and bread sounds hollow when tapped.

Per serving: 60 calories, 2 g protein, 13 g carbohydrate, 0 g total fat (0 g saturated), 0 mg cholesterol, 162 mg sodium, 52 mg potassium.

Seven-Grain Bread

1 Pound	Ingredients	1-1/2 Pound
1/3 cup	water	2/3 cup
1/4 cup	applesauce	1/3 cup
1	egg	1
1 cup	whole wheat flour	1-3/4 cups
2/3 cup	bread flour	3/4 cup
2 teaspoons	gluten flour	1 tablespoon
1/3 cup	seven-grain cereal	1/2 cup
1 tablespoon	honey	2 tablespoons
3/4 teaspoon	salt	1 teaspoon
1 teaspoon	active dry yeast	1 teaspoon

Select loaf size. Add ingredients to machine according to manufacturer's directions.

Per serving: 64 calories, 2 g protein, 13 g carbohydrate, 1 g total fat (0 g saturated), 13 mg cholesterol, 107 mg sodium, 55 mg potassium.

GRANOLA WHEAT BREAD

1 Pound	Ingredients	1-1/2 Pound
1/2 cup	pear nectar	3/4 cup
1/2 cup	milk	3/4 cup
1-1/2 teaspoons	margarine *or* butter	2 teaspoons
1-1/3 cups	whole wheat flour	2 cups
2/3 cup	bread flour	1 cup
1/3 cup	low-fat granola	1/2 cup
2 tablespoons	toasted wheat germ	3 tablespoons
1 tablespoon	gluten flour	4 teaspoons
2 teaspoons	brown sugar	1 tablespoon
1/2 teaspoon	salt	3/4 teaspoon
1/4 teaspoon	finely shredded lemon peel	1/2 teaspoon
1 teaspoon	active dry yeast	1 teaspoon
1/4 cup	dark raisins	1/3 cup

Select loaf size. Add ingredients to machine according to manufacturer's directions. Use the light setting, if available.

Per serving: 89 calories, 3 g protein, 17 g carbohydrate, 1 g total fat (0 g saturated), 1 mg cholesterol, 81 mg sodium, 99 mg potassium.

Pumpkin Seed Bread

1 Pound	Ingredients	1-1/2 Pound
1 cup	milk	1-1/2 cups
1 tablespoon	margarine *or* butter	4 teaspoons
1-2/3 cups	bread flour	2-1/4 cups
1 cup	whole wheat flour	1-1/2 cups
1/3 cup	toasted chopped pumpkin seeds	1/2 cup
1 tablespoon	brown sugar	4 teaspoons
1/2 teaspoon	salt	3/4 teaspoon
1 teaspoon	active dry yeast	1 teaspoon

Select loaf size. Add ingredients to machine according to manufacturer's directions.

Per serving: 100 calories, 4 g protein, 18 g carbohydrate, 2 g total fat (0 g saturated), 1 mg cholesterol, 84 mg sodium, 87 mg potassium.

MULTI-GRAIN HONEY WHEAT BREAD

1 Pound	Ingredients	1-1/2 Pound
3/4 cup	milk	1 cup
1	egg	1
1 tablespoon	margarine *or* butter	2 tablespoons
1 cup	bread flour	1-1/2 cups
3/4 cup	whole wheat flour	1 cup
1/3 cup	multi-grain cereal with rolled rye, oats, barley, and wheat	1/2 cup
1/3 cup	chopped walnuts	1/2 cup
1 tablespoon	toasted wheat germ	2 tablespoons
1 tablespoon	honey *or* brown sugar	2 tablespoons
1/2 teaspoon	salt	3/4 teaspoon
1 teaspoon	active dry yeast	1 teaspoon

Select loaf size. Add ingredients to machine according to manufacturer's directions.

Per serving: 94 calories, 4 g protein, 14 g carbohydrate, 3 g total fat (0 g saturated), 14 mg cholesterol, 87 mg sodium, 82 mg potassium.

WHOLE GRAIN SUNFLOWER BREAD

1 Pound	Ingredients	1-1/2 Pound
1 cup	milk	1-1/2 cups
1 tablespoon	cooking oil	2 tablespoons
1-2/3 cups	bread flour	2-1/2 cups
1/2 cup	rye flour	3/4 cup
1/2 cup	whole wheat flour	3/4 cup
1 tablespoon	honey	1 tablespoon
1/2 teaspoon	salt	3/4 teaspoon
1 teaspoon	active dry yeast	1 teaspoon
2 tablespoons	dark raisins	3 tablespoons
2 tablespoons	shelled sunflower seeds	3 tablespoons

Select loaf size. Add ingredients to machine according to manufacturer's directions.

Per serving: 105 calories, 3 g protein, 19 g carbohydrate, 2 g total fat (0 g saturated), 1 mg cholesterol, 75 mg sodium, 81 mg potassium.

HERB BREADS

Caraway Seed Whole Wheat Bread

1 Pound	Ingredients	1-1/2 Pound
3/4 cup	milk	1 cup
2 teaspoons	cooking oil	1 tablespoon
2/3 cup	whole wheat flour	1 cup
1-1/3 cups	bread flour	2 cups
1 teaspoon	honey	1-1/2 teaspoons
2 tablespoons	shelled sunflower seeds	3 tablespoons
1 teaspoon	toasted sesame seed	1-1/2 teaspoons
1 teaspoon	caraway seed, crushed*	1-1/2 teaspoons
1/2 teaspoon	salt	3/4 teaspoon
1 teaspoon	active dry yeast	1 teaspoon

Select loaf size. Add ingredients to machine according to manufacturer's directions.

*Note: If you like, substitute crushed anise seed, crushed fennel seed, or poppy seed for the caraway seed.

Per serving: 78 calories, 3 g protein, 13 g carbohydrate, 2 g total fat (0 g saturated), 1 mg cholesterol, 73 mg sodium, 60 mg potassium.

CORIANDER HONEY GRAIN BREAD

1 Pound	Ingredients	1-1/2 Pound
3/4 cup	milk	1-1/4 cups
1	egg	1
2 teaspoons	margarine *or* butter	1 tablespoon
1-1/2 cups	bread flour	2-1/2 cups
3/4 cup	whole wheat flour	1 cup
2 teaspoons	honey	1 tablespoon
3/4 teaspoon	ground coriander	1 teaspoon
1/2 teaspoon	salt	3/4 teaspoon
1/4 teaspoon	ground cinnamon	1/2 teaspoon
1/8 teaspoon	ground cloves	1/4 teaspoon
Dash	ground ginger	1/8 teaspoon
1 teaspoon	active dry yeast	1 teaspoon

Select loaf size. Add ingredients to machine according to manufacturer's directions.

Per serving: 84 calories, 3 g protein, 15 g carbohydrate, 1 g total fat (0 g saturated), 14 mg cholesterol, 83 mg sodium, 63 mg potassium.

DILL ONION WHEAT BREAD

1 Pound	Ingredients	1-1/2 Pound
1/3 cup	water	1/2 cup
1	egg	1
1/2 cup	cream-style cottage cheese, undrained	3/4 cup
2 teaspoons	margarine *or* butter	1 tablespoon
1 cup	whole wheat flour	1-1/2 cups
1 cup	bread flour	1-1/2 cups
1-1/2 teaspoons	sugar	2 teaspoons
2 teaspoons	minced dried onion	1 tablespoon
1-1/2 teaspoons	dried dillweed	2 teaspoons
1/2 teaspoon	salt	3/4 teaspoon
1 teaspoon	active dry yeast	1 teaspoon

Select loaf size. Add ingredients to machine according to manufacturer's directions.

Per serving: 77 calories, 4 g protein, 13 g carbohydrate, 1 g total fat (0 g saturated), 14 mg cholesterol, 109 mg sodium, 59 mg potassium.

FENNEL AND GRAIN BEER BREAD

1 Pound	Ingredients	1-1/2 Pound
3/4 cup	beer	1-1/4 cups
4 teaspoons	Dijon-style mustard	2 tablespoons
2 teaspoons	cooking oil	1 tablespoon
1-1/4 cups	whole wheat flour	2 cups
1 cup	bread flour	1-1/2 cups
2 teaspoons	sugar	1 tablespoon
1/2 teaspoon	garlic salt	3/4 teaspoon
1/2 teaspoon	fennel seed	3/4 teaspoon
1 teaspoon	active dry yeast	1 teaspoon

Select loaf size. Add ingredients to machine according to manufacturer's directions.

Per serving: 77 calories, 2 g protein, 14 g carbohydrate, 1 g total fat (0 g saturated), 0 mg cholesterol, 103 mg sodium, 55 mg potassium.

Garden Herb Cheese Bread

1 Pound	Ingredients	1-1/2 Pound
3/4 cup	milk	1-1/4 cups
1/4 cup	grated Parmesan cheese	1/3 cup
1/4 cup	shredded sharp cheddar cheese	1/3 cup
2 cups	bread flour	3 cups
2 teaspoons	sugar	1 tablespoon
3/4 teaspoon	onion salt	1 teaspoon
1/2 teaspoon	dried dillweed	3/4 teaspoon
1/2 teaspoon	snipped fresh basil *or*	3/4 teaspoon
1/4 teaspoon	dried basil, crushed	1/2 teaspoon
1/4 teaspoon	snipped fresh rosemary *or*	1/2 teaspoon
1/8 teaspoon	dried rosemary, crushed	1/4 teaspoon
1 teaspoon	active dry yeast	1 teaspoon

Select loaf size. Add ingredients to machine according to manufacturer's directions.

Per serving: 85 calories, 4 g protein, 14 g carbohydrate, 1 g total fat (1 g saturated), 6 mg cholesterol, 192 mg sodium, 53 mg potassium.

PESTO BREAD

1 Pound	Ingredients	1-1/2 Pound
2/3 cup	buttermilk	1 cup
1/4 cup	dry white wine	1/3 cup
2 tablespoons	grated Parmesan cheese	3 tablespoons
2 tablespoons	pesto	3 tablespoons
2-1/4 cups	bread flour	3-1/3 cups
1 clove	garlic, minced	2 cloves
2 teaspoons	sugar	1 tablespoon
1/2 teaspoon	salt	3/4 teaspoon
1 teaspoon	active dry yeast	1 teaspoon

Select loaf size. Add ingredients to machine according to manufacturer's directions.

Per serving: 85 calories, 3 g protein, 16 g carbohydrate, 1 g total fat (0 g saturated), 1 mg cholesterol, 93 mg sodium, 65 mg potassium.

OREGANO AND MOZZARELLA CHEESE BREAD

1 Pound	Ingredients	1-1/2 Pound
2/3 cup	milk	1 cup
1	egg	1
1/3 cup	shredded mozzarella cheese	1/2 cup
1/2 cup	whole wheat flour	3/4 cup
1-1/2 cups	bread flour	2-1/4 cups
1 tablespoon	sugar	4 teaspoons
1 tablespoon	snipped fresh oregano *or*	4 teaspoons
1 teaspoon	dried oregano, crushed	1-1/2 teaspoons
1/2 teaspoon	salt	3/4 teaspoon
1 teaspoon	active dry yeast	1 teaspoon

Select loaf size. Add ingredients to machine according to manufacturer's directions.

Per serving: 86 calories, 4 g protein, 14 g carbohydrate, 2 g total fat (1 g saturated), 17 mg cholesterol, 101 mg sodium, 57 mg potassium.

HERB ONION MONKEY BREAD

1 Pound	Ingredients	1-1/2 Pound
1/2 cup	water	3/4 cup
1/3 cup	dairy sour cream	1/2 cup
1-1/2 teaspoons	margarine *or* butter	2 teaspoons
1/4 cup	finely chopped onion	1/3 cup
2-1/4 cups	bread flour	3-1/3 cups
1 tablespoon	sugar	4 teaspoons
1/2 teaspoon	salt	3/4 teaspoon
1 teaspoon	active dry yeast	1 teaspoon
2 tablespoons	margarine *or* butter, melted	3 tablespoons
1 teaspoon	dried Italian seasoning, crushed	1-1/2 teaspoons

Select loaf size. Add the first 8 ingredients to machine according to manufacturer's dough cycle directions. When cycle is complete, remove dough from machine.

On a lightly floured surface, cut 1-pound dough into 32 pieces; cut 1-1/2-pound dough into 48 pieces. Combine the 2 or 3 tablespoons melted margarine and Italian seasoning. Dip the top of each dough piece into the herb-butter mixture.

Layer pieces, butter side down, in a greased oven-proof 6-cup ring mold for 1-pound dough or a 12-cup fluted tube pan for 1-1/2-pound dough. Let rise for 30 to 45 minutes or till nearly double.

Bake in a 375° oven till brown, allowing 15 to 20 minutes for small ring and 20 to 25 minutes for large ring. Invert bread onto a serving dish. Serve warm.

Per serving: 100 calories, 2 g protein, 15 g carbohydrate, 3 g total fat (1 g saturated), 0 mg cholesterol, 93 mg sodium, 38 mg potassium.

SOUTHERN FRANCE ROSEMARY BREAD

1 Pound	Ingredients	1-1/2 Pound
3/4 cup	milk	1-1/4 cups
1 tablespoon	olive oil	4 teaspoons
2 cups	bread flour	3 cups
2 tablespoons	cornmeal	3 tablespoons
2 teaspoons	sugar	1 tablespoon
1 teaspoon	snipped fresh rosemary *or*	1-1/2 teaspoons
1/2 teaspoon	dried rosemary, crushed	3/4 teaspoon
1/2 teaspoon	salt	3/4 teaspoon
1/4 teaspoon	coarsely ground black pepper	1/2 teaspoon
Dash	bottled hot pepper sauce	Dash
1 teaspoon	active dry yeast	1 teaspoon

Select loaf size. Add ingredients to machine according to manufacturer's directions.

Per serving: 82 calories, 3 g protein, 14 g carbohydrate, 1 g total fat (0 g saturated), 1 mg cholesterol, 73 mg sodium, 41 mg potassium.

SAGE AND PEPPER BREAD WITH DRIED TOMATOES

1 Pound	Ingredients	1-1/2 Pound
3/4 cup	milk	1-1/2 cups
2 teaspoons	margarine *or* butter	1 tablespoon
2 tablespoons	oil-packed dried tomatoes, drained and snipped	3 tablespoons
2-1/4 cups	bread flour	3-1/3 cups
1-1/2 teaspoons	sugar	2 teaspoons
1-1/2 teaspoons	dried sage, crushed	2 teaspoons
1/2 teaspoon	salt	3/4 teaspoon
1/2 to 3/4 teaspoon	coarsely ground pepper	3/4 to 1 teaspoon
1 teaspoon	active dry yeast	1 teaspoon

Select loaf size. Add ingredients to machine according to manufacturer's directions.

Per serving: 82 calories, 3 g protein, 15 g carbohydrate, 1 g total fat (0 g saturated), 1 mg cholesterol, 79 mg sodium, 50 mg potassium.

Turkey Stuffing Bread

1 Pound	Ingredients	1-1/2 Pound
2/3 cup	milk	1 cup
1	egg	1
1/4 cup	finely chopped onion	1/3 cup
1 tablespoon	margarine *or* butter	1 tablespoon
2 cups	bread flour	3 cups
1/4 cup	cornmeal	1/3 cup
1-1/2 teaspoons	brown sugar	2 teaspoons
1 teaspoon	celery seed	1-1/2 teaspoons
1/2 teaspoon	salt	3/4 teaspoon
1/2 teaspoon	dried sage, crushed	3/4 teaspoon
1/2 teaspoon	poultry seasoning	3/4 teaspoon
1/4 teaspoon	pepper	1/2 teaspoon
1 teaspoon	active dry yeast	1 teaspoon

Select loaf size. Add ingredients to machine according to manufacturer's directions.

Per serving: 90 calories, 3 g protein, 15 g carbohydrate, 2 g total fat (0 g saturated), 14 mg cholesterol, 85 mg sodium, 52 mg potassium.

VEGETABLE BREADS

Broccoli Cheese Bread

1 Pound	Ingredients	1-1/2 Pound
1/2 cup	fresh *or* frozen chopped broccoli	3/4 cup
3 tablespoons	finely chopped onion	1/4 cup
1 tablespoon	margarine *or* butter	4 teaspoons
2/3 cup	milk	1 cup
1	egg	1
1/4 cup	grated Parmesan cheese	1/3 cup
2 cups	bread flour	3 cups
1/2 teaspoon	salt	3/4 teaspoon
1 teaspoon	active dry yeast	1 teaspoon

Select loaf size. If using frozen broccoli, thaw and drain well. In a skillet cook broccoli and onion in margarine or butter till tender, stirring occasionally. Cool slightly.

Add broccoli mixture and remaining ingredients to machine according to manufacturer's directions.

Per serving: 80 calories, 3 g protein, 13 g carbohydrate, 2 g total fat (0 g saturated), 14 mg cholesterol, 85 mg sodium, 52 mg potassium.

Carrot Herb Bread

1 Pound	Ingredients	1-1/2 Pound
2/3 cup	milk	1 cup
1-1/2 teaspoons	margarine *or* butter	1 tablespoon
3/4 cup	finely shredded carrot	1 cup
1-1/3 cups	whole wheat flour	2 cups
2/3 cup	bread flour	1 cup
1 tablespoon	honey	2 tablespoons
1 teaspoon	poppy seed (optional)	2 teaspoons
1/2 teaspoon	salt	3/4 teaspoon
1/2 teaspoon	dried dillweed	3/4 teaspoon
1/2 teaspoon	dried thyme, crushed	3/4 teaspoon
1/2 teaspoon	dried parsley flakes	3/4 teaspoon
1 teaspoon	active dry yeast	1 teaspoon

Select loaf size. Add ingredients to machine according to manufacturer's directions.

Per serving: 72 calories, 3 g protein, 14 g carbohydrate, 1 g total fat (0 g saturated), 1 mg cholesterol, 79 mg sodium, 88 mg potassium.

MEXICAN-STYLE CORNBREAD

1 Pound	Ingredients	1-1/2 Pound
2/3 cup	canned cream-style corn	1 cup
3 tablespoons	water	1/4 cup
1/4 cup	salsa	1/3 cup
1/4 cup	shredded cheddar cheese	1/3 cup
2 tablespoons	cooking oil	3 tablespoons
2-1/4 cups	bread flour	3-1/3 cups
1/3 cup	cornmeal	3/4 cup
1/2 of a medium	jalapeño pepper,* rinsed, seeded, and finely chopped (optional)	1 medium
1/4 teaspoon	salt	1/2 teaspoon
1 teaspoon	active dry yeast	1 teaspoon

Select loaf size. Add ingredients to machine according to manufacturer's directions.

*Note: Because chili peppers contain volatile oils that can burn skin and eyes, avoid direct contact with peppers as much as possible. Wear plastic or rubber gloves or work under cold running water. If your bare hands touch the chili peppers, wash your hands well with soap and water.

Per serving: 111 calories, 3 g protein, 18 g carbohydrate, 3 g total fat (1 g saturated), 2 mg cholesterol, 116 mg sodium, 49 mg potassium.

Potato Chive Bread

1 Pound	Ingredients	1-1/2 Pound
1/3 cup	shredded, unpeeled potato	1/2 cup
2 teaspoons	margarine *or* butter	1 tablespoon
1 cup	milk	1-1/2 cups
2-1/2 cups	bread flour	3-3/4 cups
2 tablespoons	snipped fresh chives	3 tablespoons
2 teaspoons	sugar	1 tablespoon
1/2 teaspoon	salt	3/4 teaspoon
1 teaspoon	active dry yeast	1 teaspoon

Select loaf size. In a medium skillet cook potato in hot margarine or butter till tender and brown. Add potatoes and remaining ingredients to machine according to manufacturer's directions.

Per serving: 95 calories, 3 g protein, 18 g carbohydrate, 1 g total fat (0 g saturated), 1 mg cholesterol, 81 mg sodium, 75 mg potassium.

POTATO HERB WHEAT BREAD

1 Pound	Ingredients	1-1/2 Pound
1/2 cup	water	3/4 cup
1/2 cup	chopped, peeled potato	3/4 cup
	milk	
1 tablespoon	cooking oil	1 tablespoon
1-1/3 cups	bread flour	2 cups
2/3 cup	whole wheat flour	1 cup
2 tablespoons	nonfat dry milk powder	3 tablespoons
1 tablespoon	honey	4 teaspoons
1/2 teaspoon	salt	3/4 teaspoon
1/4 teaspoon	dried thyme, crushed	1/2 teaspoon
1/4 teaspoon	dried oregano, crushed	1/2 teaspoon
1/4 teaspoon	dried rosemary, crushed	1/4 teaspoon
1 teaspoon	active dry yeast	1 teaspoon

Select loaf size. In a small saucepan combine water and potato. Bring to boiling; reduce heat. Cook, covered, about 8 minutes or till potato is very tender. Do not drain. Mash potato in the water; measure mixture. Add enough milk to make 3/4 cup for the 1-pound loaf or 1-1/4 cups for the 1-1/2-pound loaf.

Add potato mixture and other ingredients to machine according to manufacturer's directions.

Per serving: 80 calories, 3 g protein, 15 g carbohydrate, 1 g total fat (0 g saturated), 0 mg cholesterol, 73 mg sodium, 90 mg potassium.

Fall Sweet Potato Bread

1 Pound	Ingredients	1-1/2 Pound
1/2 cup	water	3/4 cup
1/3 cup	chopped, peeled sweet potatoes	1/2 cup
1 tablespoon	margarine *or* butter	4 teaspoons
2 cups	bread flour	3 cups
2 tablespoons	nonfat dry milk	3 tablespoons
2 teaspoons	brown sugar	1 tablespoon
1/2 teaspoon	salt	3/4 teaspoon
1 teaspoon	active dry yeast	1 teaspoon

Select loaf size. In a small saucepan combine water and sweet potato. Bring to boiling; reduce heat. Cover and simmer about 15 minutes or till tender. Do not drain. Mash potato in the water. Measure potato mixture. Add enough water to make 3/4 cup for the 1-pound loaf or 1-1/4 cups for the 1-1/2-pound loaf. Cool slightly to 120°.

Add sweet potato mixture and remaining ingredients to machine according to manufacturer's directions.

Per serving: 76 calories, 2 g protein, 14 g carbohydrate, 1 g total fat (0 g saturated), 0 mg cholesterol, 81 mg sodium, 45 mg potassium.

TOMATO BREAD

1 Pound	Ingredients	1-1/2 Pound
3/4 cup	vegetable juice cocktail	1 cup + 2 tablespoons
2 tablespoons	grated Parmesan cheese	3 tablespoons
1 tablespoon	cooking oil	4 teaspoons
1-1/3 cups	bread flour	2 cups
2/3 cup	whole wheat flour	1 cup
1 tablespoon	honey	4 teaspoons
1 tablespoon	snipped fresh tarragon *or* basil, *or*	4 teaspoons
3/4 teaspoon	dried tarragon *or* basil, crushed	1 teaspoon
1/2 teaspoon	salt	3/4 teaspoon
1 teaspoon	active dry yeast	1 teaspoon

Select loaf size. Add ingredients to machine according to manufacturer's directions.

Per serving: 77 calories, 3 g protein, 14 g carbohydrate, 1 g total fat (0 g saturated), 1 mg cholesterol, 123 mg sodium, 58 mg potassium.

Sweet Potato Bread

1 Pound	Ingredients	1-1/2 Pound
1/3 cup	milk	1/2 cup
1	egg	1
1/2 cup	mashed, drained, canned sweet potatoes	3/4 cup
1 tablespoon	cooking oil	2 tablespoons
1-1/3 cups	bread flour	2 cups
2/3 cup	whole wheat flour	1 cup
1 tablespoon	brown sugar	2 tablespoons
1/4 cup	tiny marshmallows	1/3 cup
1/2 teaspoon	salt	3/4 teaspoon
1 teaspoon	active dry yeast	1 teaspoon

Select loaf size. Add ingredients to machine according to manufacturer's directions. Use the light setting, if available.

Per serving: 89 calories, 3 g protein, 16 g carbohydrate, 2 g total fat (0 g saturated), 14 mg cholesterol, 75 mg sodium, 68 mg potassium.

VEGETABLE BREAD

1 Pound	Ingredients	1-1/2 Pound
1/2 cup	finely shredded zucchini, lightly packed	2/3 cup
1/4 cup	finely shredded carrot, lightly packed	1/3 cup
1/2 cup	milk	3/4 cup
1 tablespoon	cooking oil	2 tablespoons
1-2/3 cups	bread flour	2-1/2 cups
1/2 cup	whole wheat flour	3/4 cup
1/4 cup	regular rolled oats, toasted*	1/3 cup
1/4 cup	chopped walnuts	1/3 cup
1 tablespoon	honey	2 tablespoons
1/2 teaspoon	salt	3/4 teaspoon
1/4 teaspoon	ground cinnamon	1/2 teaspoon
1 teaspoon	active dry yeast	1 teaspoon

Select loaf size. Add ingredients to machine according to manufacturer's directions.

*Note: For directions on toasting oats, see page 34.

Per serving: 98 calories, 3 g protein, 16 g carbohydrate, 2 g total fat (0 g saturated), 1 mg cholesterol, 72 mg sodium, 76 mg potassium.

FRUIT, NUT, & SPICE BREADS

SUNFLOWER AND GRAINS BREAD

1 Pound	Ingredients	1-1/2 Pound
3/4 cup	buttermilk	1 cup + 2 tablespoons
2 teaspoons	cooking oil	1 tablespoon
1-1/3 cups	bread flour	2 cups
1/3 cup	whole wheat flour	1/2 cup
1/3 cup	regular rolled oats, toasted*	1/2 cup
2 tablespoons	honey *or* molasses	2 tablespoons
1/2 teaspoon	salt	3/4 teaspoon
1 teaspoon	active dry yeast	1 teaspoon
1/3 cup	shelled sunflower seeds	1/2 cup
3 tablespoons	dark raisins	1/4 cup

Select loaf size. Add all ingredients to machine according to manufacturer's directions.

*Note: For directions on toasting oats, see page 34.

Per serving: 97 calories, 3 g protein, 16 g carbohydrate, 2 g total fat (0 g saturated), 0 mg cholesterol,
80 mg sodium, 86 mg potassium.

ALMOND BREAD

1 Pound	Ingredients	1-1/2 Pound
3/4 cup	milk	1-1/4 cups
1-1/2 teaspoons	shortening	2 teaspoons
1-1/3 cups	bread flour	2 cups
2/3 cup	whole wheat flour	1 cup
1/4 cup	sliced almonds	1/3 cup
2 teaspoons	sugar	1 tablespoon
1/2 teaspoon	salt	3/4 teaspoon
1 teaspoon	active dry yeast	1 teaspoon

Select loaf size. Add ingredients to machine according to manufacturer's directions.

Per serving: 79 calories, 3 g protein, 13 g carbohydrate, 2 g total fat (0 g saturated), 1 mg cholesterol, 77 mg sodium, 66 mg potassium.

ALLSPICE BREAD

1 Pound	Ingredients	1-1/2 Pound
3/4 cup	apple juice	1-1/4 cups
1 tablespoon	cooking oil	4 teaspoons
2 cups	bread flour	3 cups
1/3 cup	regular rolled oats, toasted*	1/2 cup
3 tablespoons	packed brown sugar	1/4 cup
1/2 teaspoon	salt	3/4 teaspoon
1/2 teaspoon	ground allspice	3/4 teaspoon
1 teaspoon	active dry yeast	1 teaspoon
1/4 cup	dark raisins	1/3 cup

Select loaf size. Add ingredients to machine according to manufacturer's directions.

*Note: For directions on toasting oats, turn to page 34.

Per serving: 93 calories, 2 g protein, 18 g carbohydrate, 1 g total fat (0 g saturated), 0 mg cholesterol, 135 mg sodium, 65 mg potassium.

ANISE BREAD

1 Pound	Ingredients	1-1/2 Pound
1/3 cup	milk	1/2 cup
1/3 cup	orange juice	1/2 cup
1	egg	1
1 tablespoon	margarine *or* butter	2 tablespoons
2 cups	bread flour	3 cups
1 tablespoon	brown sugar	4 teaspoons
1 teaspoon	aniseed	1-1/2 teaspoons
1/2 teaspoon	salt	3/4 teaspoon
1/2 teaspoon	finely shredded lemon peel	3/4 teaspoon
1/2 teaspoon	finely shredded orange peel	3/4 teaspoon
Dash	ground mace	1/8 teaspoon
Dash	ground nutmeg	1/8 teaspoon
1 teaspoon	active dry yeast	1 teaspoon

Select loaf size. Add ingredients to machine according to manufacturer's directions.

Per serving: 82 calories, 3 g protein, 14 g carbohydrate, 1 g total fat (0 g saturated), 14 mg cholesterol, 82 mg sodium, 48 mg potassium.

Chunky Apple Bread

1 Pound	Ingredients	1-1/2 Pound
3/4 cup	apple juice	1-1/4 cups
1/2 cup	finely chopped, peeled apple	3/4 cup
1 tablespoon	margarine *or* butter	2 tablespoons
1-1/4 cups	bread flour	2 cups
1 cup	whole wheat flour	1-1/2 cups
1/2 cup	regular rolled oats	3/4 cup
2 teaspoons	sugar	1 tablespoon
1/2 teaspoon	salt	3/4 teaspoon
1/2 teaspoon	ground cinnamon	1/2 teaspoon
1 teaspoon	active dry yeast	1 teaspoon
1/4 cup	chopped walnuts	1/3 cup
1/4 cup	dark raisins (optional)	1/3 cup

Select loaf size. Add ingredients to machine according to manufacturer's directions.

Per serving: 109 calories, 3 g protein, 19 g carbohydrate, 2 g total fat (0 g saturated), 0 mg cholesterol, 76 mg sodium, 99 mg potassium.

SPICY APPLE BREAD

1 Pound	Ingredients	1-1/2 Pound
1/2 cup	apple juice	3/4 cup
1/4 cup	applesauce	1/3 cup
1 tablespoon	margarine *or* butter	4 teaspoons
1-1/4 cups	bread flour	2 cups
3/4 cup	whole wheat flour	1 cup
2 teaspoons	honey	1 tablespoon
1 teaspoon	ground cinnamon	1-1/2 teaspoons
1/2 teaspoon	salt	3/4 teaspoon
1 teaspoon	active dry yeast	1 teaspoon

Select loaf size. Add ingredients to machine according to manufacturer's directions.

Per serving: 74 calories, 2 g protein, 14 g carbohydrate, 1 g total fat (0 g saturated), 0 mg cholesterol, 76 mg sodium, 50 mg potassium.

BANANA-NUT OATMEAL BREAD

1 Pound	Ingredients	1-1/2 Pound
1/2 cup	buttermilk	2/3 cup
1/3 cup	mashed ripe banana	1/2 cup
1	egg	1
1 tablespoon	margarine *or* butter	2 tablespoons
1-1/3 cups	bread flour	2 cups
3/4 cup	whole wheat flour	1 cup + 2 tablespoons
1/4 cup	rolled oats, toasted*	1/3 cup
1 tablespoon	honey	4 teaspoons
1/2 teaspoon	salt	3/4 teaspoon
1/2 teaspoon	ground cinnamon	3/4 teaspoon
1/4 teaspoon	ground nutmeg	1/4 teaspoon
1 teaspoon	active dry yeast	1 teaspoon
1/4 cup	chopped walnuts	1/3 cup

Select loaf size. Add ingredients to machine according to manufacturer's directions. Use the light setting, if available.

*Note: For directions on toasting oats, turn to page 34.

Per serving: 100 calories, 4 g protein, 16 g carbohydrate, 3 g total fat (0 g saturated), 14 mg cholesterol, 88 mg sodium, 88 mg potassium.

CARDAMOM SPICE BREAD

1 Pound	Ingredients	1-1/2 Pound
1/2 cup	water	3/4 cup
1/4 cup	shredded apple	1/3 cup
2 teaspoons	margarine *or* butter	1 tablespoon
1 cup	bread flour	1-1/2 cups
1 cup	whole wheat flour	1-1/2 cups
1 tablespoon	honey	2 tablespoons
1 teaspoon	finely shredded orange peel	1-1/2 teaspoons
1/2 teaspoon	salt	3/4 teaspoon
1/2 teaspoon	ground cardamom	1/2 teaspoon
1 teaspoon	active dry yeast	1 teaspoon
1/4 cup	dark raisins (optional)	1/3 cup

Select loaf size. Add ingredients to machine according to manufacturer's directions.

Per serving: 73 calories, 2 g protein, 15 g carbohydrate, 1 g total fat (0 g saturated), 0 mg cholesterol, 73 mg sodium, 64 mg potassium.

CINNAMON RAISIN BREAD

1 Pound	Ingredients	1-1/2 Pound
3/4 cup	milk	1 cup + 2 tablespoons
2 teaspoons	margarine *or* butter	1 tablespoon
2 cups	bread flour	3 cups
2 teaspoons	brown sugar	1 tablespoon
1/2 teaspoon	salt	3/4 teaspoon
1 teaspoon	ground cinnamon	1-1/2 teaspoons
1 teaspoon	active dry yeast	1 teaspoon
1/2 cup	dark raisins	3/4 cup

Select loaf size. Add ingredients to machine according to manufacturer's directions.

Per serving: 90 calories, 3 g protein, 18 g carbohydrate, 1 g total fat (0 g saturated), 1 mg cholesterol, 80 mg sodium, 83 mg potassium.

DATE-GRANOLA BREAD

1 Pound	Ingredients	1-1/2 Pound
1 cup	buttermilk	1-1/4 cups
1 tablespoon	margarine *or* butter	1 tablespoon
1-1/4 cups	bread flour	2 cups
1 cup	whole wheat flour	1-1/2 cups
1/2 cup	granola	2/3 cup
1 tablespoon	honey	2 tablespoons
1/2 teaspoon	salt	3/4 teaspoon
1 teaspoon	active dry yeast	1 teaspoon
1/4 cup	chopped pecans	1/3 cup
1/4 cup	chopped pitted dates	1/3 cup

Select loaf size. Add ingredients to machine according to manufacturer's directions. Use the light setting, if available.

Per serving: 116 calories, 3 g protein, 20 g carbohydrate, 3 g total fat (1 g saturated), 1 mg cholesterol, 99 mg sodium, 106 mg potassium.

LEMON PECAN BREAD

1 Pound	Ingredients	1-1/2 Pound
1/2 cup	milk	3/4 cup
1/4 cup	dairy sour cream	1/3 cup
1	egg	1
1 tablespoon	margarine *or* butter	1 tablespoon
2-1/4 cups	bread flour	3-1/2 cups
2 tablespoons	sugar	3 tablespoons
1/2 teaspoon	salt	3/4 teaspoon
1/2 teaspoon	finely shredded lemon peel	3/4 teaspoon
1 teaspoon	active dry yeast	1 teaspoon
1/2 cup	toasted chopped pecans	3/4 cup

Select loaf size. Add ingredients to machine according to manufacturer's directions. Use the light setting, if available.

Per serving: 173 calories, 4 g protein, 31 g carbohydrate, 4 g total fat (1 g saturated), 14 mg cholesterol, 86 mg sodium, 51 mg potassium.

Sherried Date Bread

1 Pound	Ingredients	1-1/2 Pound
2/3 cup	white grape juice	1 cup
3 tablespoons	dry sherry	1/4 cup
1 tablespoon	margarine *or* butter	4 teaspoons
2 cups	bread flour	3 cups
1/4 cup	toasted chopped pecans	1/3 cup
1/2 teaspoon	salt	3/4 teaspoon
1/8 teaspoon	ground cinnamon	1/4 teaspoon
1 teaspoon	active dry yeast	1 teaspoon
1/3 cup	snipped, pitted dates	1/2 cup

Select loaf size. Add ingredients to machine according to manufacturer's directions.

Per serving: 101 calories, 2 g protein, 17 g carbohydrate, 2 g total fat (0 g saturated), 0 mg cholesterol, 76 mg sodium, 67 mg potassium.

Raisin-Pumpernickel Bread

1 Pound	Ingredients	1-1/2 Pound
3/4 cup + 2 tablespoons	milk	1-1/3 cups
2 teaspoons	cooking oil	1 tablespoon
1-1/3 cups	bread flour	2 cups
2/3 cup	whole wheat flour	1 cup
1/3 cup	rye flour	1/2 cup
1 tablespoon	gluten flour	1 tablespoon
1 tablespoon	unsweetened cocoa powder	2 tablespoons
1 tablespoon	molasses	2 tablespoons
1 teaspoon	caraway seed	1-1/2 teaspoons
1/2 teaspoon	salt	3/4 teaspoon
1 teaspoon	active dry yeast	1 teaspoon
1/4 cup	dark raisins	1/3 cup

Select loaf size. Add ingredients to machine according to manufacturer's directions.

Per serving: 91 calories, 3 g protein, 17 g carbohydrate, 1 g total fat (0 g saturated), 1 mg cholesterol, 76 mg sodium, 128 mg potassium.

DESSERT BREADS

DOUBLE CHOCOLATE BREAD

1 Pound	Ingredients	1-1/2 Pound
2/3 cup	milk	1 cup
1 teaspoon	vanilla	1-1/2 teaspoons
1	egg	1
1 tablespoon	margarine *or* butter	1 tablespoon
2 cups	bread flour	3 cups
2 tablespoons	brown sugar	3 tablespoons
1 tablespoon	unsweetened cocoa powder	4 teaspoons
1/2 teaspoon	salt	3/4 teaspoon
1 teaspoon	active dry yeast	1 teaspoon
1/2 cup	semisweet chocolate pieces	2/3 cup

Select loaf size. Add ingredients to machine according to manufacturer's directions.

Mexican Double Chocolate Bread: For 1-pound loaf, add 1/4 teaspoon ground cinnamon with the flour. For a 1-1/2-pound loaf, add 1/2 teaspoon ground cinnamon.

Per serving: 119 calories, 3 g protein, 20 g carbohydrate, 3 g total fat (0 g saturated), 14 mg cholesterol, 90 mg sodium, 87 mg potassium.

Apple Strudel Bread

1 Pound	Ingredients	1-1/2 Pound
1/2 cup	milk	3/4 cup
1	egg	1
1/4 cup	margarine *or* butter	1/3 cup
2 cups + 2 tablespoons	bread flour	3-1/4 cups
1/4 cup	sugar	1/3 cup
1/2 teaspoon	salt	3/4 teaspoon
1 teaspoon	active dry yeast	1 teaspoon
2 tablespoons	margarine *or* butter, softened	3 tablespoons
2 cups	thinly sliced, peeled apples	3 cups
1/3 cup	packed brown sugar	1/2 cup
1/3 cup	dark raisins	1/2 cup
1 tablespoon	all-purpose flour	4 teaspoons
1/2 teaspoon	ground cinnamon	1 teaspoon
1/3 cup	sifted powdered sugar	1/2 cup
1 to 2 teaspoons	milk	2 to 3 teapoons

Select loaf size. Add the first 7 ingredients to machine according to manufacturer's directions. Select dough cycle. When cycle is complete, remove dough from machine, cover and let rest 10 minutes.

Grease a 10x15x1-inch baking pan; set aside. On a lightly floured surface, roll 1-pound dough into a 12x18-inch rectangle; roll 1-1/2-pound dough into a 12x24-inch rectangle. Brush dough with the softened margarine.

For filling, in a small mixing bowl, combine apples, brown sugar, raisins, 3 to 4 teaspoons flour, and cinnamon. Beginning about 2 inches from a long side, spoon filling in a 3-inch-wide band across dough. Starting from the long side, carefully roll up dough; pinch edges and ends to seal. Carefully transfer to prepared baking pan, curving dough to fit and form a crescent shape. Cover and let rise in warm place about 45 minutes or till nearly double.

Bake in a 350° oven for 30 to 35 minutes or till brown; cover with foil for the last 10 to 15 minutes to prevent overbrowning, if necessary. Remove from pan. Cool on a rack.

For icing, in a small mixing bowl stir together powdered sugar and 1 to 3 teaspoons milk. Add enough milk to make an icing of drizzling consistency. Drizzle over strudel.

Per serving: 168 calories, 3 g protein, 28 g carbohydrate, 5 g total fat (1 g saturated), 14 mg cholesterol, 127 mg sodium, 95 mg potassium.

Chocolate-Cream Cheese Bread

1 Pound	Ingredients	1-1/2 Pound
1/2 cup	milk	3/4 cup
2 ounces	light cream cheese (neufchâtel)	3 ounces
1	egg	1
2-1/4 cups	bread flour	3-1/3 cups
2 tablespoons	brown sugar	3 tablespoons
1/2 teaspoon	salt	3/4 teaspoon
1 teaspoon	active dry yeast	1 teaspoon
4 ounces	light cream cheese (neufchâtel), softened	6 ounces
1/4 cup	sifted powdered sugar	1/3 cup
1	egg yolk	1
2 teaspoons	all-purpose flour	1 tablespoon
1/4 cup	semisweet chocolate pieces	1/3 cup
1/2 cup	chopped walnuts (optional)	3/4 cup

Select loaf size. Add the first 7 ingredients to machine according to manufacturer's directions. Select dough cycle. When the cycle is complete, remove dough from machine. Cover and let rest 10 minutes.

Meanwhile, for filling, stir together 4 ounces (6 ounces for the 1-1/2-pound loaf) softened cream cheese, powdered sugar, egg yolk, and all-purpose flour. Set aside.

For the 1-pound recipe, on a lightly floured surface, roll dough to a 12x8-inch rectangle. Place on a greased baking sheet. Spread filling in a 4-inch-wide strip lengthwise down the center of dough. Sprinkle chocolate pieces and, if desired, nuts over cream cheese mixture. Using a sharp knife, slit dough at 1-inch intervals along each side of filling to within 1/2-inch of filling. Fold strips diagonally over filling, alternating from side to side. Cover and let rise in a warm place for 30 minutes or till nearly double.

Bake in 350° oven for 25 to 30 minutes or till golden brown. Cool slightly on a wire rack. If desired, brush with Coffee Glaze. Serve warm or cool. Makes 12 servings.

For the 1-1/2-pound recipe, divide the dough in half. Roll half of the dough at a time to a 9x8-inch rectangle. Fill, cut, and continue as above. Makes 18 servings.

Coffee Glaze: In a small bowl stir together 1/2 cup sifted *powdered sugar* and enough *coffee liqueur* or *coffee* (2 to 4 teaspoons) to make a mixture of glazing consistency.

Per serving: 220 calories, 7 g protein, 28 g carbohydrate, 9 g total fat (3 g saturated), 48 mg cholesterol, 162 mg sodium, 119 mg potassium.

CHOCOLATE-STRAWBERRY BREAD

1 Pound	Ingredients	1-1/2 Pound
1-2/3 cups	fresh strawberries	3 cups
2 tablespoons	margarine *or* butter	3 tablespoons
2 tablespoons	brown sugar	3 tablespoons
1 tablespoon	unsweetened cocoa powder	4 teaspoons
1/4 teaspoon	salt	1/2 teaspoon
2 cups	bread flour	3 cups
2 tablespoons	nonfat dry milk powder	3 tablespoons
1 teaspoon	active dry yeast	1 teaspoon
3 tablespoons	miniature semisweet chocolate pieces	1/4 cup

Select loaf size. Place strawberries in a blender container or food processor bowl. Cover and blend or process till smooth. Measure 1 cup for 1-pound loaf or 1 1/2 cups for 1 1/2-pound loaf. Add strawberries and remaining ingredients to machine according to manufacturer's directions.

Note: If desired, serve with ice cream and fresh strawberries. Drizzle melted semisweet chocolate on top.

Per serving: 105 calories, 3 g protein, 18 g carbohydrate, 3 g total fat (0 g saturated), 0 mg cholesterol, 54 mg sodium, 77 mg potassium.

German Chocolate Bread

1 Pound	Ingredients	1-1/2 Pound
2/3 cup	milk	1 cup
1	egg	1
1 tablespoon	margarine *or* butter	2 tablespoons
1-1/3 cups	bread flour	2 cups
2/3 cup	whole wheat flour	1 cup
2 tablespoons	brown sugar	3 tablespoons
4 teaspoons	unsweetened cocoa powder	2 tablespoons
1/2 teaspoon	salt	3/4 teaspoon
1 teaspoon	active dry yeast	1 teaspoon
1/3 cup	semisweet chocolate pieces	1/2 cup
1/4 cup	chopped nuts	1/3 cup
1/4 cup	toasted coconut	1/3 cup

Select loaf size. Add ingredients to machine according to manufacturer's directions. Use the light setting, if available.

Per serving: 128 calories, 4 g protein, 18 g carbohydrate, 5 g total fat (1 g saturated), 15 mg cholesterol, 94 mg sodium, 97 mg potassium.

Holiday Spirit Bread

1 Pound	Ingredients	1-1/2 Pound
1/3 cup	dark raisins	1/2 cup
2 tablespoons	bourbon, cream sherry, *or* orange liqueur	3 tablespoons
1/2 cup	milk	2/3 cup
1	egg	1
1 tablespoon	margarine *or* butter	2 tablespoons
2 cups	bread flour	3 cups
2 tablespoons	brown sugar	3 tablespoons
1/2 teaspoon	salt	3/4 teaspoon
1/4 teaspoon	ground nutmeg	1/2 teaspoon
1 teaspoon	active dry yeast	1 teaspoon
1 teaspoon	finely shredded orange peel	1-1/2 teaspoons

Select loaf size. Soak raisins in bourbon or liqueur for 30 minutes. Pour off any excess liquid; add to other liquid ingredients.

Add all ingredients, except raisins, to machine according to manufacturer's directions. Add raisins at raisin setting. Use the light setting, if available.

Per serving: 98 calories, 3 g protein, 18 g carbohydrate, 1 g total fat (0 g saturated), 14 mg cholesterol, 84 mg sodium, 65 mg potassium.

ORANGE-SHERRY BREAD

1 Pound	Ingredients	1-1/2 Pound
2/3 cup	milk	1 milk
2 tablespoons	dry sherry	3 tablespoons
1 tablespoon	margarine *or* butter	2 tablespoons
1 cup	bread flour	1-1/2 cups
1 cup	whole wheat flour	1-1/2 cups
2 tablespoons	honey	3 tablespoons
1-1/2 teaspoons	finely shredded orange peel	2 teaspoons
1/2 teaspoon	salt	3/4 teaspoon
1 teaspoon	active dry yeast	1 teaspoon
1/3 cup	dark raisins	1/2 cup

Select loaf size. Combine ingredients according to manufacturer's directions. Use the light setting, if available.

Per serving: 88 calories, 3 g protein, 17 g carbohydrate, 1 g total fat (0 g saturated), 1 mg cholesterol, 81 mg sodium, 84 mg potassium.

ROLLS & SHAPED BREADS

BRIOCHE

1 Pound	Ingredients	1-1/2 Pound
1/4 cup	milk	1/3 cup
2	eggs	3
3 tablespoons	margarine *or* butter	1/4 cup
2-1/4 cups	bread flour	3-1/3 cups
2 tablespoons	sugar	3 tablespoons
1/2 teaspoon	salt	3/4 teaspoon
1 teaspoon	active dry yeast	1 teaspoon
1	beaten egg	1
1 tablespoon	sugar	1 tablespoon

Select loaf size. Add the first 7 ingredients to machine according to manufacturer's directions. Select dough cycle. When cycle is complete, remove dough from machine and divide into 4 portions. Cover and let rest for 10 minutes.

Shape 3 portions into 4 or 6 balls each, making a total of 12 or 18 balls; set aside.

Shape the remaining portion into 12 or 18 small balls. Place large balls of dough in greased 2-1/2-inch muffin pans or 3-inch fluted individual brioche pans. Press dough in the center. Brush with water. Press the small ball into indentation. Let rise in a warm place about 40 minutes or till nearly double.

Stir together egg and 1 tablespoon sugar; brush onto tops. Bake in a 375° oven for 12 to 15 minutes or till golden. If desired, brush again with egg mixture after 10 minutes. Cool on a wire rack.

Per serving: 151 calories, 5 g protein, 22 g carbohydrate, 5 g total fat (1 g saturated), 54 mg cholesterol, 141 mg sodium, 54 mg potassium.

CREAMY CARAMEL ROLLS

1 Pound	Ingredients	1-1/2 Pound
2/3 cup	milk	1 cup
1	egg	1
1 tablespoon	margarine *or* butter	2 tablespoons
2-1/2 cups	bread flour	3-3/4 cups
3 tablespoons	sugar	1/3 cup
1 teaspoon	finely shredded orange peel (optional)	1-1/2 teaspoons
1/2 teaspoon	salt	3/4 teaspoon
1 teaspoon	active dry yeast	1 teaspoon
1/4 cup	margarine *or* butter, softened	1/3 cup
1/2 cup	packed brown sugar	2/3 cup
2 tablespoons	light corn syrup	3 tablespoons
1/4 cup	finely chopped pecans	1/3 cup
1/2 cup	whipping cream	3/4 cup

Select loaf size. Add the first 8 ingredients to machine according to manufacturer's directions. Select dough cycle. When the cycle is complete, remove dough from machine. Cover and let rest for 10 minutes.

Meanwhile, in a small mixing bowl stir together the softened margarine or butter, brown sugar, corn syrup, and pecans; set aside.

For the 1-pound recipe, on a lightly floured surface, roll dough into a 16x12-inch rectangle. Spread with brown sugar mixture to within 1/2 inch of edges. Starting from a long side, roll up jelly-roll style; seal edge. Cut into sixteen 1-inch-thick slices. Place, cut side down, in a greased 9x9x2-inch baking pan. Cover; let rise in a warm place about 30 minutes or till nearly double. Pour whipping cream over rolls. Bake in a 350° oven about 35 minutes or till brown. Cool in pan on a wire rack about 5 minutes. Invert onto a serving plate; serve warm. Makes 16 rolls.

For the 1-1/2-pound recipe, divide the dough in half. Roll half of the dough at a time to a 12-inch square. Fill, roll, cut and continue as above, making 24 rolls total and using a 13x9x2-inch baking pan. Makes 24 rolls.

Per serving: 196 calories, 4 g protein, 28 g carbohydrate, 8 g total fat (2 g saturated), 23 mg cholesterol, 124 mg sodium, 84 mg potassium.

Wheat Cinnamon Rolls

1 Pound	Ingredients	1-1/2 Pound
1/2 cup	milk	3/4 cup
1	egg	1
1 tablespoon	margarine *or* butter	2 tablespoons
1-1/3 cups	bread flour	2 cups
2/3 cup	whole wheat flour	1 cup
2 tablespoons	packed brown sugar	3 tablespoons
1/2 teaspoon	salt	3/4 teaspoon
1 teaspoon	active dry yeast	1 teaspoon
1/2 cup	packed brown sugar	2/3 cup
3 tablespoons	melted margarine *or* butter	1/4 cup
1 tablespoon	light corn syrup	2 tablespoons
3 tablespoons	packed brown sugar	1/4 cup
1-1/2 teaspoons	ground cinnamon	2 teaspoons
1/3 cup	raisins (optional)	1/2 cup
2 tablespoons	margarine *or* butter, softened	3 tablespoons

Select loaf size. Add the first 8 ingredients to machine according to manufacturer's directions. Select dough cycle. When cycle is complete, remove dough from machine. Cover and let rest for 10 minutes.

Meanwhile, for glaze, in a small saucepan combine 1/2 cup brown sugar, (2/3 cup for 1-1/2-pound loaf) 3 tablespoons margarine or butter (1/4 cup for 1-1/2-pound loaf), and corn syrup. Heat on medium heat till margarine or butter is melted and ingredients are combined.

For filling, combine 3 tablespoons brown sugar (1/4 cup for 1-1/2-pound loaf), the cinnamon, and, if desired, raisins.

For the 1-pound recipe, spread the glaze evenly in a 9x9x2-inch baking pan. Set aside. On a lightly floured surface, roll the dough into a 12x8-inch rectangle. Spread with softened margarine. Sprinkle with filling. Starting from a long side, roll up jelly-roll style; seal edge. Cut into twelve 1-inch-thick slices. Place, cut side down, in prepared pan. Cover; let rise in a warm place about 30 minutes or till nearly double. Bake in a 375° oven about 25 minutes or till golden brown. Cool in pan on a wire rack about 5 minutes; invert onto a serving plate. Serve warm. Makes 12 rolls.

For the 1-1/2-pound recipe, spread the glaze in one 13x9x2-inch baking pan or two 8x1-1/2-inch round baking pans. Roll the dough into an 18x8-inch rectangle. Fill, roll, and cut as above, making 18 rolls total. Place, cut side down, in prepared pan. Cover; let rise in a warm place about 45 to 60 minutes or till nearly double. Bake and serve as directed above. Makes 18 rolls.

Per serving: 213 calories, 4 g protein, 35 g carbohydrate, 7 g total fat (1 g saturated), 19 mg cholesterol, 173 mg sodium, 152 mg potassium.

BREADSTICKS

1 Pound	Ingredients	1-1/2 Pound
2/3 cup	milk	1 cup
1 tablespoon	cooking oil	2 tablespoons
2 cups	bread flour	3 cups
1 tablespoon	sugar	2 tablespoons
1/2 teaspoon	salt	3/4 teaspoon
1 teaspoon	active dry yeast	1 teaspoon
1	egg white	1
1 tablespoon	water	1 tablespoon
	sesame seed, poppy seed, caraway seed,	
	coarse salt, *or* grated Parmesan cheese	

Select loaf size. Add ingredients to machine according to manufacturer's directions.

Select dough cycle. When cycle is complete, remove dough from machine. Cover and let rest for 10 minutes.

Grease a baking sheet; set aside. On a lightly floured surface, divide 1-pound dough into 24 pieces; divide 1-1/2-pound dough into 32 pieces. Roll each piece into an 8-inch-long rope.

Arrange ropes on prepared baking sheet. Stir together egg white and water; brush onto breadsticks. Sprinkle with desired seed, salt, or Parmesan cheese. Bake in a 350° oven for 15 to 20 minutes or till golden. Cool on a wire rack. Serve warm or cool. Makes 24 or 32 breadsticks.

Per serving: 52 calories, 2 g protein, 9 g carbohydrate, 1 g total fat (0 g saturated), 0 mg cholesterol, 48 mg sodium, 24 mg potassium.

FOCACCIA

1 Pound	Ingredients	1-1/2 Pound
3/4 cup	milk	1 cup
1 tablespoon	olive oil	2 tablespoons
2 cups	bread flour	3 cups
1 teaspoon	dried oregano, crushed	2 teaspoons
1/2 teaspoon	salt	3/4 teaspoon
1 teaspoon	active dry yeast	1 teaspoon
	nonstick spray coating	
2 tablespoons	olive oil	3 tablespoons
1 clove	garlic, minced	1 clove
1/3 cup	grated Parmesan cheese	1/2 cup
3 tablespoons	snipped fresh parsley	1/4 cup

Select loaf size. Add the first 6 ingredients to machine according to manufacturer's directions. Select dough cycle. When cycle is complete, remove dough from machine. Cover and let rest for 10 minutes.

Spray nonstick coating onto a 12-inch pizza pan for 1-pound dough or a 15x10x1-inch baking pan for 1-1/2-pound dough. Using your hands, gently stretch and press dough to fit evenly into the pan. Cover and let rise in warm place for 30 to 40 minutes or till nearly double.

With two fingers, poke holes all over the dough. In a medium mixing bowl, stir together 2 or 3 tablespoons olive oil and garlic; drizzle over dough. Sprinkle with Parmesan cheese and parsley. Bake in a 400° oven for 25 to 30 minutes or till brown. Cool on a wire rack. Serve warm or cool.

Per serving: 101 calories, 3 g protein, 13 g carbohydrate, 4 g total fat (1 g saturated), 2 mg cholesterol, 112 mg sodium, 46 mg potassium.

Wheat, Rosemary, and Tomato Focaccia

1 Pound	Ingredients	1-1/2 Pound
3/4 cup	milk	1-1/4 cups
1 tablespoon	olive oil	2 tablespoons
1-1/2 cups	whole wheat flour	2-1/4 cups
1/2 cup	bread flour	3/4 cup
1/4 cup	cornmeal	1/3 cup
2 tablespoons	snipped oil-packed dried tomatoes	3 tablespoons
1 teaspoon	dried oregano, crushed	1-1/2 teaspoons
1/2 teaspoon	salt	3/4 teaspoon
1 teaspoon	active dry yeast	1 teaspoon
2 tablespoons	olive oil	3 tablespoons
1 clove	garlic, minced	1 clove
1/4 cup	grated Parmesan cheese	1/3 cup
2 teaspoons	snipped fresh rosemary *or*	1 tablespoon
1/2 teaspoon	dried rosemary, crushed	1 teaspoon

Select loaf size. Add first 9 ingredients to machine according to manufacturer's directions. Select dough cycle. When cycle is complete, remove dough from machine. (If making a 1-1/2-pound loaf, divide dough in half.) Cover; let dough rest 10 minutes.

Grease an 11- to 13-inch pizza pan for 1-pound dough. For 1-1/2-pound dough grease a 15x10x1-inch baking pan or two 11- to 13-inch pizza pans. Cover and let rise in a warm place for 30 to 40 minutes or till nearly double. With 2 fingers, poke holes all over dough. Combine 2 or 3 tablespoons olive oil and garlic; drizzle over dough. Sprinkle with Parmesan cheese and rosemary. Bake in a 400° oven for 25 to 30 minutes or till golden brown. Cool on a wire rack. Serve warm or cool. Makes 16 or 24 servings.

Per serving: 98 calories, 3 g protein, 14 g carbohydrate, 4 g total fat (1 g saturated), 2 mg cholesterol, 103 mg sodium, 85 mg potassium.

ENGLISH MUFFINS

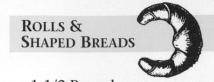

1 Pound	Ingredients	1-1/2 Pound
3/4 cup	milk	1 cup
1/4 cup	regular farina	1/3 cup
1-3/4 cups	bread flour	2-2/3 cups
1 tablespoon	corn syrup	2 tablespoons
1/2 teaspoon	salt	3/4 teaspoon
1 teaspoon	active dry yeast	1 teaspoon
	nonstick spray coating	
	cornmeal	

Select loaf size. Add all ingredients except cornmeal to machine according to manufacturer's directions. Select dough cycle. When cycle is complete, remove dough from machine. Cover and let rest for 10 minutes.

Spray a baking sheet with nonstick coating; sprinkle with cornmeal. On a lightly floured surface, roll the dough to 1/2-inch thickness. Using a 3- or 4-inch round cookie cutter, cut dough into circles. Place rounds on the prepared baking sheet. Cover dough and let rise in a warm place for 45 minutes.

Sprinkle dough with additional cornmeal, if desired. On a lightly greased griddle or nonstick skillet, cook English muffins over medium heat for 4 to 5 minutes on each side till golden brown. Cool on a wire rack. Makes 6 to 8 muffins from 1 pound; 9 to 12 muffins from 1-1/2 pound.

Cinnamon-Raisin English Muffins: For a 1-pound loaf, add 1/2 teaspoon *ground cinnamon* with the flour and 1/4 cup dark *raisins* at the raisin setting. For a 1-1/2-pound loaf add 1/2 teaspoon *ground cinnamon* and 1/2 cup dark *raisins*.

Per serving: 181 calories, 6 g protein, 35 g carbohydrate, 1 g total fat (0 g saturated), 2 mg cholesterol, 196 mg sodium, 100 mg potassium.

PITA BREAD

1 Pound	Ingredients	1-1/2 Pound
3/4 cup	milk	1-1/4 cups
1 tablespoon	olive oil	2 tablespoons
2 cups	bread flour	3 cups
1 teaspoon	sugar	1-1/2 teaspoons
1/2 teaspoon	salt	3/4 teaspoon
1 teaspoon	active dry yeast	1 teaspoon

Select loaf size. Add ingredients to machine according to manufacturer's directions. Select dough cycle. When cycle is complete, remove dough from machine. Cover and let rest for 10 minutes.

For 1-pound dough, divide dough into 7 portions; for 1-1/2 -pound dough, divide dough into 10 portions. Shape each portion into a smooth ball. On a lightly floured surface, use a rolling pin to roll each ball into a 6-inch circle. Cover dough and let rise about 30 minutes or till slightly puffed.

On a greased baking sheet arrange 2 to 3 dough rounds. Bake in a 450° oven for 5 to 7 minutes or till bread is puffed and tops are beginning to brown, turning once after 3 minutes. Remove from oven. Cool on a wire rack. Repeat with remaining dough. To serve, cut pita rounds in half and fill with filling or wrap bread around filling. Makes 7 to 10 pita bread rounds.

Whole Wheat Pita Bread: Make as directed above, except for 1-pound dough, substitute 1 cup bread flour and 1 cup whole wheat flour for the 2 cups bread flour. For 1-1/2-pound dough, substitute 1-1/2 cups bread flour and 1-1/2 cups whole wheat flour for the 3 cups bread flour.

Per serving: 175 calories, 6 g protein, 30 g carbohydrate, 3 g total fat (1 g saturated), 2 mg cholesterol, 166 mg sodium, 87 mg potassium.

HAMBURGER WHEAT BUNS

1 Pound	Ingredients	1-1/2 Pound
2/3 cup	milk	1 cup
1 tablespoon	margarine *or* butter	4 teaspoons
1-1/4 cups	whole wheat flour	2 cups
3/4 cup	bread flour	1 cup
1 tablespoon	honey	4 teaspoons
1/2 teaspoon	salt	3/4 teaspoon
1 teaspoon	active dry yeast	1 teaspoon
1	beaten egg	1
	sesame seed *or* poppy seed	

Select loaf size. Add the first 7 ingredients to machine according to manufacturer's directions. Select dough cycle. When cycle is complete, remove dough from machine. Cover and let rest for 10 minutes.

For 1-pound dough, divide into 4 balls; for 1-1/2-pound dough, divide into 6 balls. Make bun shapes. Place on greased baking sheets, 4 inches apart. Flatten to 3-1/2-inch rounds. Cover and let rise till nearly double (about 1 hour). Brush tops with beaten egg; sprinkle with sesame seed or poppy seed. Bake in a 375° oven for 12 to 15 minutes or till done. Cool on a wire rack. Makes 4 or 6 buns.

Seasoned Hamburger Wheat Buns: For 1-pound dough, add 1 teaspoon *sesame seed, poppy seed, snipped fresh chives,* or *dried minced onion* along with rest of dough ingredients. For 1-1/2-pound dough, add 2 teaspoons *sesame seed, poppy seed, snipped fresh chives,* or *dried minced onion.*

Per serving: 71 calories, 2 g protein, 13 g carbohydrate, 1 g total fat (0 g saturated), 1 mg cholesterol, 81 mg sodium, 64 mg potassium.

Whole Wheat and Cheese Pizza Dough

1 Pound	Ingredients	1-1/2 Pound
2/3 cup	water	1 cup
1/3 cup	shredded reduced-fat mozzarella cheese	1/2 cup
4 teaspoons	olive oil	2 tablespoons
1 cup	bread flour	1-1/2 cups
1 cup	whole wheat flour	1-1/2 cups
1 teaspoon	dried thyme, basil, *or* oregano, crushed	1-1/4 teaspoons
1/2 teaspoon	salt	3/4 cup
1 teaspoon	active dry yeast	1 teaspoon
	cornmeal	

Select loaf size. Add all ingredients except cornmeal to machine according to manufacturer's directions. Select dough setting. When cycle is complete, remove dough from machine.

If making 1-1/2-pound dough, divide dough in half. If desired, freeze half to use another time. Wrap it in plastic wrap and transfer to a freezer bag. Seal, label, and freeze for up to 3 months. To thaw, let dough stand at room temperature about 2-1/2 hours or till thawed. Or, thaw overnight in the refrigerator.

For each thin pizza, grease a 12-inch pizza pan or large baking sheet. If desired, sprinkle with cornmeal. On a lightly floured surface, roll one portion of dough into a 13-inch circle. Transfer to pan or baking sheet. Do not let dough rise. Bake in a 425° oven about 12 minutes or till light brown. Top with pizza sauce and toppings of your choice. Bake for 10 to 15 minutes more or till bubbly.

For each pan pizza, grease a 9x9x2-inch baking pan. If desired, sprinkle with cornmeal. With greased fingers, pat one portion of dough onto the bottom and halfway up the sides of prepared pan. Cover and let rise in a warm place for 30 to 45 minutes or till nearly double. Bake in a 375° oven for 20 to 25 minutes or till light brown. Top with pizza sauce and toppings of your choice. Bake for 15 to 20 minutes more or till bubbly. Makes 1 or 2 crusts, 4 servings each.

Pizza Topping Combinations:
- Crumbled blue cheese, low-fat Canadian-style bacon, thinly sliced red onion.
- Brie or Camembert cheese and pecans or walnuts.
- Chunky salsa and Monterey Jack or cheddar cheese

Per serving: 324 calories, 14 g protein, 48 g carbohydrate, 9 g total fat (3 g saturated), 12 mg cholesterol, 370 mg sodium, 201 mg potassium.

WHOLE WHEAT DINNER ROLLS

1 Pound	Ingredients	1-1/2 Pound
2/3 cup	milk	1 cup
1/4 cup	cracked wheat	1/3 cup
1	egg	1
2 tablespoons	margarine *or* butter	3 tablespoons
1-1/2 cups	whole wheat flour	2 cups
1/2 cup	bread flour	1 cup
2 tablespoons	maple syrup	3 tablespoons
1/2 teaspoon	salt	3/4 teaspoon
1 teaspoon	active dry yeast	1 teaspoon
	nonstick spray coating	
	melted margarine *or* butter	

Select loaf size. Bring milk to boiling. Add cracked wheat; let stand about 5 minutes or till slightly cool. Add the first 9 ingredients to machine according to manufacturer's directions. Select dough cycle. When cycle is complete, remove dough from machine. Cover and let rest for 10 minutes. Shape according to directions on opposite page.

Bowknots: Spray a baking sheet with nonstick spray coating; set aside. For 1-pound dough, divide dough into 16 portions; for 1-1/2-pound dough, divide dough into 24 portions. With floured hands, roll each portion into a 6-inch-long rope. Tie loosely into a knot. Arrange on prepared baking sheet. Bake as directed below. Makes 16 or 24 rolls.

Cloverleaf Rolls: Spray muffin pans with nonstick spray coating; set aside. For 1-pound dough, divide into 16 portions; for 1-1/2-pound dough, divide into 24 portions. Divide each portion into thirds; shape each into smooth 1-inch balls. Dip into melted margarine or butter, then place balls in each muffin cup. Bake as directed below. Makes 16 or 24 rolls.

Fantans: Spray muffin pans with nonstick spray coating; set aside. On a lightly floured surface, roll out 1-pound dough to a 12-inch square; roll out 1-1/2-pound dough to a 12x18-inch rectangle. Brush with 1 tablespoon melted margarine or butter. Cut dough into 1-inch-wide strips. Stack 6 strips on top of one another; cut stacked strips into 1-1/2-inch pieces. Place each stack in each prepared muffin cup. Bake as directed below. Makes 16 or 24 rolls.

Parker House Rolls: Spray a baking sheet with nonstick spray coating; set aside. On a lightly floured surface, roll out dough to 1/4 inch thickness. Brush with melted margarine or butter. Cut into 2-1/2- to 3-inch circles. Use the dull edge of a table knife to make an off-center crease in each round. Fold along the crease; place 2 to 3 inches apart on prepared baking sheet so the large half is on top. Bake as directed below. Makes 16 or 24 rolls.

After shaping any of the rolls above, let rise in a warm place about 30 minutes or till nearly double. Bake in a 375° oven for 12 to 15 minutes or till golden brown. Remove from pans; brush with additional melted margarine or butter, if desired. Cool slightly on a wire rack. Serve warm or cool.

Per serving: 98 calories, 3 g protein, 15 g carbohydrate, 3 g total fat (1 g saturated), 14 mg cholesterol, 35 mg sodium, 88 mg potassium.

Soft Whole Wheat Pretzels

1 Pound	Ingredients	1-1/2 Pound
2/3 cup	milk	1 cup
1 tablespoon	margarine *or* butter	2 tablespoons
1-1/2 cups	whole wheat flour	2-1/4 cups
1/2 cup	bread flour	3/4 cup
2 teaspoons	sugar	1 tablespoon
1/2 teaspoon	salt	3/4 teaspoon
1 teaspoon	active dry yeast	1 teaspoon
2 teaspoons	salt	2 teaspoons
	sesame seed, poppy seed, *and/or* coarse salt	

Select loaf size. Add the first 7 ingredients to machine according to manufacturer's directions for dough cycle. When cycle is complete, remove and punch down dough. Turn out onto a lightly floured surface. Cover and let rise for 10 minutes.

Grease 2 baking sheets; set aside. For 1-pound dough, divide dough into 8 portions; for 1-1/2-pound dough, divide dough into 12 portions. Gently pull each strip into a rope about 16 inches long. Shape into pretzels. Place pretzels 1/2 inch apart on the prepared baking sheets. Bake in a 475° oven for 4 minutes. Remove from oven. Reduce oven temperature to 350°.

Meanwhile, dissolve 2 teaspoons salt in 2 quarts boiling water. Reduce heat. Gently slide pretzels, a few at a time, into simmering water. Simmer for 2 minutes, turning once. Remove with a slotted spoon and drain on wire rack. Place 1/2 inch apart on well-greased baking sheets. If desired, sprinkle with sesame seed, poppy seed, or coarse salt. Bake in the 350° oven for 20 to 25 minutes or till golden brown. Cool on a wire rack. Makes 8 or 12 pretzels.

Per serving: 135 calories, 5 g protein, 25 g carbohydrate, 2 g total fat (1 g saturated), 1 mg cholesterol, 161 mg sodium, 138 mg potassium.

INTERNATIONAL BREADS

AMERICAN AMARANTH BREAD

1 Pound	Ingredients	1-1/2 Pound
3/4 cup	milk	1 cup + 2 tablespoons
1	egg white	1
2 teaspoons	cooking oil	1 tablespoon
2 cups	bread flour	3 cups
1/3 cup	amaranth flour	1/2 cup
1 tablespoon	honey	2 tablespoons
1 teaspoon	vanilla	1-1/2 teaspoons
1/2 teaspoon	salt	3/4 teaspoon
1 teaspoon	active dry yeast	1 teaspoon
1/3 cup	chopped walnuts (optional)	1/2 cup

Select loaf size. Add ingredients to machine according to manufacturer's directions.

Per serving: 128 calories, 5 g protein, 17 g carbohydrate, 5 g total fat (1 g saturated), 1 mg cholesterol, 76 mg sodium, 87 mg potassium.

ARMENIAN FLATBREAD

1 Pound	Ingredients	1-1/2 Pound
3/4 cup	milk	1 cup + 2 tablespoons
2 tablespoons	olive oil	3 tablespoons
2 cups	bread flour	3 cups
2 teaspoons	sugar	1 tablespoon
1/2 teaspoon	salt	3/4 teaspoon
1 teaspoon	active dry yeast	1 teaspoon
2 tablespoons	milk	3 tablespoons
2 teaspoons	sesame seed	1 tablespoon

Select loaf size. Add the first 6 ingredients to machine according to manufacturer's directions. Select dough cycle. When cycle is complete, remove dough from machine. Cover and let rest for 10 minutes.

Divide 1-pound dough in half; divide 1-1/2-pound loaf into thirds. On a lightly floured surface, roll each portion into a 14-inch circle. Transfer to large greased baking sheets. Using a fork, prick the surface of each cracker several times. Brush crackers with 2 to 3 tablespoons milk; sprinkle sesame seed on top. Bake in a 400° oven for 10 to 12 minutes or till light brown. Cool on a wire rack.

Per serving: 88 calories, 3 g protein, 14 g carbohydrate, 2 g total fat (0 g saturated), 1 mg cholesterol, 74 mg sodium, 43 mg potassium.

Scottish Baps

1 Pound	Ingredients	1-1/2 Pound
1/2 cup	milk	3/4 cup
1	egg	1
2 tablespoons	margarine *or* butter	3 tablespoons
2 cups	bread flour	3 cups
1 tablespoon	sugar	4 teaspoons
1/2 teaspoon	salt	3/4 teaspoon
1 teaspoon	active dry yeast	1 teaspoon
1 tablespoon	margarine *or* butter, melted	2 tablespoons
	preserves *or* honey (optional)	

Select dough amount. Add the first 7 ingredients to machine according to manufacturer's directions. Select dough cycle. When cycle is complete, remove dough from machine.

On a lightly floured surface, divide 1-pound dough into 8 portions; divide 1-1/2-pound dough into 12 portions. Roll out each piece or flatten with hands into 4-inch rounds. Arrange the rounds on a greased baking sheet. Let rest for 10 minutes.

Brush dough with melted margarine or butter. Bake in a 400° oven for 10 to 12 minutes or till golden brown. Cool slightly on a wire rack. Serve warm with preserves or honey, if desired. Makes 8 or 12 baps.

Per serving: 185 calories, 6 g protein, 27 g carbohydrate, 6 g total fat (1 g saturated), 28 mg cholesterol, 199 mg sodium, 74 mg potassium.

WHOLE WHEAT IRISH BREAD

1 Pound	Ingredients	1-1/2 Pound
3/4 cup	buttermilk	1-1/4 cups
1 tablespoon	cooking oil	2 tablespoons
1 cup	bread flour	1-1/2 cups
1 cup	whole wheat flour	1-1/2 cups
2 tablespoons	brown sugar	3 tablespoons
1/2 teaspoon	salt	3/4 teaspoon
2 teaspoons	caraway seed	1 tablespoon
1 teaspoon	active dry yeast	1 teaspoon
1/2 cup	dark raisins	2/3 cup

Select loaf size. Add ingredients to machine according to manufacturer's directions.

Per serving: 92 calories, 3 g protein, 18 g carbohydrate, 1 g total fat (0 g saturated), 0 mg cholesterol, 80 mg sodium, 108 mg potassium.

Limpa (Swedish Sweet Rye Bread)

1 Pound	Ingredients	1-1/2 Pound
3/4 cup + 2 tablespoons	water	1-1/2 cups
1 tablespoon	margarine *or* butter	2 tablespoons
1-1/2 cups	bread flour	2-2/3 cups
3/4 cup	rye flour	1 cup
1 tablespoon	honey	4 teaspoons
1 teaspoon	finely shredded orange peel	1-1/2 teaspoons
1/2 teaspoon	salt	3/4 teaspoon
1/2 teaspoon	caraway seed	3/4 teaspoon
1/4 teaspoon	fennel seed	1/2 teaspoon
1 teaspoon	active dry yeast	1 teaspoon

Select loaf size. Add ingredients to machine according to manufacturer's directions.

Per serving: 75 calories, 2 g protein, 14 g carbohydrate, 1 g total fat (0 g saturated), 0 mg cholesterol, 76 mg sodium, 35 mg potassium.

Russian Wheat and Rye Bread

1 Pound	Ingredients	1-1/2 Pound
1 cup	milk	1-1/4 cups
2 teaspoons	vinegar	1 tablespoon
2 teaspoons	shortening	1 tablespoon
1-1/4 cups	bread flour	2 cups
3/4 cup	rye flour	1 cup
3/4 cup	whole wheat flour	1 cup
1 tablespoon	gluten flour	2 tablespoons
1 tablespoon	unsweetened cocoa powder	4 teaspoons
1 tablespoon	molasses	2 tablespoons
1 teaspoon	caraway seed	1-1/2 teaspoons
1/2 teaspoon	salt	3/4 teaspoon
1/4 teaspoon	fennel seed	1/2 teaspoon
1 teaspoon	active dry yeast	1 teaspoon

Select loaf size. Add ingredients to machine according to manufacturer's directions.

Per serving: 93 calories, 3 g protein, 17 g carbohydrate, 1 g total fat (0 g saturated), 1 mg cholesterol, 82 mg sodium, 121 mg potassium.

St. Lucia Buns (Saffron Buns)

1 Pound	Ingredients	1-1/2 Pound
2/3 cup	milk	1 cup
1	egg	1
3 tablespoons	margarine *or* butter	1/4 cup
2 tablespoons	brown sugar	3 tablespoons
1 teaspoon	finely shredded orange peel	1-1/2 teaspoons
1/2 teaspoon	salt	3/4 teaspoon
1/8 teaspoon	thread saffron, crushed, *or*	1/8 teaspoon
dash	ground saffron	several dashes
2 cups	bread flour	2-1/4 cups
1 teaspoon	active dry yeast	1 teaspoon
1	beaten egg	1
1 tablespoon	water	1 tablespoon
	raisins	
	sugar	

Select loaf size. Add the first 9 ingredients to machine according to manufacturer's dough cycle directions. When cycle is complete, remove dough from pan. Cover and let rest for 10 minutes. Divide 1-pound dough into 16 pieces; divide 1-1/2-pound dough into 24 pieces. On a lightly floured surface, roll each portion into a smooth 10-inch-long rope. Form each rope into an "S" shape and curve both ends in a coil. Cross 2 of these "S"-shape ropes to form an X; repeat with remaining "S"-shape ropes.

Place on a greased baking sheet. Cover; let rise about 3 minutes or till nearly double. Mix egg and water; brush onto buns. Place a raisin in the center of each coil. Sprinkle with sugar. Bake in a 375° oven about 10 minutes or till golden. Cool on a wire rack. Makes 8 or 12 buns.

Per serving: 280 calories, 8 g protein, 48 g carbohydrate, 7 g total fat (1 g saturated), 55 mg cholesterol, 213 mg sodium, 242 mg potassium.

SALLY LUNN

1 Pound	Ingredients	1-1/2 Pound
1/4 cup	evaporated milk	1/3 cup
2	eggs	3
3 tablespoons	margarine *or* butter	1/4 cup
2 cups	bread flour	3 cups
2 tablespoons	sugar	3 tablespoons
1/2 teaspoon	salt	3/4 teaspoon
1 teaspoon	active dry yeast	1 teaspoon

Select loaf size. Add ingredients to machine according to manufacturer's directions. Use the light setting, if available.

Per serving: 100 calories, 3 g protein, 15 g carbohydrate, 3 g total fat (1 g saturated), 27 mg cholesterol, 104 mg sodium, 45 mg potassium.

Pandolce (Italian Sweet Bread)

1 Pound	Ingredients	1-1/2 Pound
2/3 cup	milk	1 cup
1	egg	1
2 tablespoons	margarine *or* butter	3 tablespoons
2 cups	bread flour	3 cups
2 tablespoons	sugar	3 tablespoons
1 teaspoon	finely shredded orange peel	1 teaspoon
1/2 teaspoon	salt	3/4 teaspoon
1 teaspoon	active dry yeast	1 teaspoon
1/4 cup	toasted pinenuts	1/3 cup
1/4 cup	dark raisins	1/3 cup
1/4 cup	diced candied citron	1/3 cup
1 tablespoon	margarine *or* butter, melted	1 tablespoon
	powdered sugar	
	diced candied citron	

Select loaf size. Add the first 11 ingredients to machine according to manufacturer's directions. Select dough cycle. When cycle is complete, remove dough from machine. Cover and let rest for 10 minutes.

Grease an 8-inch springform pan for 1-pound dough or a 9-inch round pan for 1-1/2-pound dough. Press dough evenly into pan. Brush with 1 tablespoon melted margarine. Cover; let rise in a warm place about 30 minutes or till nearly double.

Bake in a 375° oven about 30 minutes or till golden brown. Cool on a wire rack. Sprinkle with powdered sugar; garnish with additional candied citron.

Per serving: 362 calories, 6 g protein, 68 g carbohydrate, 8 g total fat (1 g saturated), 28 mg cholesterol, 219 mg sodium, 123 mg potassium.

CHALLAH

1 Pound	Ingredients	1-1/2 Pound
1/2 cup	milk	3/4 cup
1	egg	2
1 tablespoon	cooking oil	2 tablespoons
2 cups	bread flour	3-1/4 cups
1 tablespoon	honey	2 tablespoons
1/2 teaspoon	salt	3/4 teaspoon
1 teaspoon	active dry yeast	1 teaspoon
1	beaten egg	1
1 teaspoon	sesame seed, poppy seed, *or* caraway seed	1-1/2 teaspoons

Select loaf size. Add the first 7 ingredients to machine according to manufacturer's directions. Select dough cycle. When the cycle is complete, remove dough from machine; cover and let rest for 10 minutes. On a lightly floured surface, divide dough into 3 equal pieces. For a 1-pound loaf, roll each piece into a 12-inch-long rope; for a 1-1/2-pound loaf, roll into 18-inch-long ropes.

Place ropes, side by side, 1 inch apart on a greased baking sheet. Starting in the middle, loosely braid by bringing left rope underneath the center rope. Then bring the right rope under the new center rope. Repeat to end. On the other end, braid to center by bringing the outside ropes alternately over center rope. Moisten and press ends together to seal; tuck under slightly. Cover and let rise in a warm place for 35 to 45 minutes or till nearly double.

Brush top with a beaten egg; sprinkle with sesame seed, poppy seed, or caraway seed. Bake in a 375° oven for 25 to 30 minutes or till done; cover with foil the last 10 minutes to prevent overbrowning, if necessary. Cool on a wire rack.

Per serving: 88 calories, 3 g protein, 14 g carbohydrate, 2 g total fat (0 g saturated), 27 mg cholesterol, 79 mg sodium, 41 mg potassium.

PORTUGUESE KING'S CAKE

1 Pound	Ingredients	1-1/2 Pound
2/3 cup	milk	1 cup
1	egg	1
1 tablespoon	margarine *or* butter	2 tablespoons
2 cups	bread flour	3 cups
2 tablespoons	sugar	3 tablespoons
1/2 teaspoon	salt	3/4 teaspoon
1 teaspoon	active dry yeast	1 teaspoon
1/3 cup	diced mixed candied fruits and peels	1/2 cup
1/4 cup	chopped walnuts	1/3 cup
1 recipe	Powdered Sugar Icing	1 recipe

Select loaf size. Add ingredients to machine according to manufacturer's directions. When cool, frost with Powdered Sugar Icing.

Powdered Sugar Icing: In a small mixing bowl stir together 1/2 cup sifted *powdered sugar* and enough *milk* (2 to 3 teaspoons) to make an icing of drizzling consistency.

Per serving: 120 calories, 3 g protein, 21 g carbohydrate, 3 g total fat (1 g saturated), 14 mg cholesterol, 85 mg sodium, 88 mg potassium.

German Christmas Stollen

1 Pound	Ingredients	1-1/2 Pound
2/3 cup	milk	1 cup
1	egg	1
1/2 teaspoon	almond extract *or* rum flavoring	3/4 teaspoon
1 tablespoon	margarine *or* butter	4 teaspoons
2 cups	bread flour	3 cups
1 tablespoon	brown sugar	4 teaspoons
1 teaspoon	finely shredded lemon peel	1-1/2 teaspoons
1 teaspoon	finely shredded orange peel	1-1/2 teaspoons
1/2 teaspoon	salt	3/4 teaspoon
1/8 teaspoon	ground mace	1/8 teaspoon
1/8 teaspoon	ground cardamom	1/8 teaspoon
1 teaspoon	active dry yeast	1 teaspoon
1/3 cup	dark raisins *or* currants	1/2 cup
1/3 cup	slivered almonds	1/2 cup
1/3 cup	diced mixed candied fruits and peels	1/2 cup

Select loaf size. Add the first 12 ingredients to machine according to manufacturer's directions. At the raisin setting, add raisins or currants, almonds, and fruits and peels. Use the light setting, if available.

Per serving: 117 calories, 3 g protein, 20 g carbohydrate, 3 g total fat (0 g saturated), 14 mg cholesterol, 85 mg sodium, 120 mg potassium.

CUBAN BREAD

1 Pound	Ingredients	1-1/2 Pound
3/4 cup	water	1 cup + 2 tablespoons
2 cups	bread flour	3 cups
1 tablespoon	cornmeal	2 tablespoons
1 teaspoon	sugar	1-1/2 teaspoons
1/2 teaspoon	salt	3/4 teaspoon
1 teaspoon	active dry yeast	1 teaspoon

Select loaf size. Add ingredients to machine according to manufacturer's directions.

Per serving: 65 calories, 2 g protein, 13 g carbohydrate, 0 g total fat (0 g saturated), 0 mg cholesterol, 67 mg sodium, 21 mg potassium.

PANETTONE

1 Pound	Ingredients	1-1/2 Pound
1/3 cup	milk	2/3 cups
3 tablespoons	sweet marsala wine *or* cream sherry	1/4 cup
1	egg	1
2 tablespoons	margarine *or* butter	3 tablespoons
1 tablespoon	honey	4 teaspoons
1 teaspoon	vanilla	1 teaspoon
2-1/4 cups	bread flour	3-1/3 cups
1 teaspoon	aniseed, crushed	1-1/2 teaspoons
1/2 teaspoon	salt	3/4 teaspoon
1/4 teaspoon	ground cloves	1/4 teaspoon
1 teaspoon	active dry yeast	1 teaspoon
1/4 cup	dark raisins	1/3 cup
1/4 cup	currants	1/3 cup
1/4 cup	diced candied citron	1/3 cup
1/4 cup	chopped pecans *or* walnuts	1/3 cup

Select loaf size. Combine all ingredients according to manufacturer's directions. Use light setting if available.

Per serving: 134 calories, 4 g protein, 22 g carbohydrate, 3 g total fat (1 g saturated), 14 mg cholesterol, 91 mg sodium, 88 mg potassium.

Hungarian Coffeecake

1 Pound	Ingredients	1-1/2 Pound
2/3 cup	buttermilk	1 cup
1	egg	1
2 tablespoons	margarine *or* butter	3 tablespoons
2-1/2 cups	bread flour	3-3/4 cups
2 tablespoons	sugar	3 tablespoons
1 teaspoon	finely shredded orange peel	1-1/2 teaspoons
1/2 teaspoon	salt	3/4 teaspoon
1 teaspoon	active dry yeast	1 teaspoon
1/3 cup	dark raisins *or* dried pitted cherries	1/2 cup
	or dried blueberries	
1/4 cup	sugar	1/3 cup
1/4 cup	toasted chopped almonds *or* pecans	1/3 cup
3/4 teaspoon	ground cinnamon	1-1/4 teaspoons
2 tablespoons	margarine *or* butter, melted	3 tablespoons

Select loaf size. Add the first 8 ingredients to machine according to manufacturer's dough cycle directions. When cycle is complete, remove dough from machine.

On a lightly floured surface, gently knead in raisins, cherries, or blueberries. Cover and let rest for 10 minutes. Lightly grease an 8-cup ring mold for 1-pound loaf or a 12-cup ring mold or fluted tube pan for the 1-1/2-pound loaf; set aside.

Divide 1-pound dough into 20 pieces; divide 1-1/2-pound dough into 30 pieces. Shape pieces of dough into smooth balls. In a small mixing bowl combine 1/4 to 1/3 cup sugar, chopped nuts, and cinnamon. Dip each ball first into melted margarine or butter, then into nut mixture. Place a layer of coated balls in the bottom of the prepared pan. Top with another layer of coated balls. Cover and let rise in a warm place for 30 to 45 minutes or till nearly double.

Bake in a 350° oven for 25 to 30 minutes or till top is light brown; cover with foil the last 10 minutes to prevent overbrowning, if necessary. Cool in pan for 1 minute. Invert onto serving plate. Serve warm.

Per serving: 144 calories, 4 g protein, 22 g carbohydrate, 5 g total fat (1 g saturated), 14 mg cholesterol, 115 mg sodium, 81 mg potassium.

STREUSEL KUCHEN

1 Pound	Ingredients	1-1/2 Pound
2/3 cup	milk	1 cup
1	egg	1
1 tablespoon	margarine *or* butter	1 tablespoon
2 cups	bread flour	3 cups
2 tablespoons	sugar	3 tablespoons
1/2 teaspoon	salt	3/4 teaspoon
1 teaspoon	active dry yeast	1 teaspoon
1/3 cup	orange marmalade *or*	1/2 cup
1/2 cup	fresh blueberries (optional)	3/4 cup
2 tablespoons	brown sugar	3 tablespoons
1 tablespoon	bread flour *or* all-purpose flour	4 teaspoons
1 tablespoon	margarine *or* butter, softened	2 tablespoons
1/2 teaspoon	ground cinnamon	3/4 teaspoon
1/3 cup	walnuts *or* almonds, chopped	1/2 cup
3/4 cup	sifted powdered sugar	1 cup
3 to 4 teaspoons	milk	4 to 5 teaspoons

Select loaf size. Add the first 7 ingredients to machine according to manufacturer's directions. Select dough cycle. When cycle is complete, remove dough from machine. Turn dough out onto a lightly floured surface. Punch down and divide dough in half. Cover and let rest for 10 minutes.

Press half of the 1-pound dough into a greased 9x1-1/2-inch round baking pan; press half of the 1-1/2-pound dough into a 9x9x2-inch square baking pan. If desired, top dough with marmalade or blueberries.

In a medium mixing bowl stir together brown sugar, the 3 or 4 teaspoons flour, 1 or 2 tablespoons margarine or butter, and cinnamon; add nuts. Sprinkle half of the nut mixture on top of dough in pan.

On a lightly floured surface, roll remaining dough into a 9-inch circle for 1-pound dough or a 9-inch square for 1-1/2-pound dough; place atop dough in pan. Sprinkle with remaining nut mixture. Cover; let rise for 30 to 40 minutes or till nearly double.

Bake in a 350° oven for 25 to 30 minutes or till golden brown; cover with foil the last 5 minutes to prevent overbrowning, if necessary. Cool on a wire rack.

For icing, stir together powdered sugar and enough of the 3 to 5 teaspoons milk to make an icing of drizzling consistency; drizzle atop coffeecake. Makes 8 or 12 servings.

Per serving: 300 calories, 7 g protein, 53 g carbohydrate, 7 g total fat (1 g saturated), 28 mg cholesterol, 190 mg sodium, 130 mg potassium.

LITHUANIAN COFFEE BREAD

1 Pound	Ingredients	1-1/2 Pound
2/3 cup	milk	1 cup
1	egg	1
1/4 teaspoon	vanilla	1/2 teaspoon
2 tablespoons	margarine *or* butter	3 tablespoons
2 cups	bread flour	3 cups
2 tablespoons	sugar	3 tablespoons
1-1/2 teaspoons	finely shredded lemon peel	2 teaspoons
1/2 teaspoon	salt	3/4 teaspoon
1 teaspoon	active dry yeast	1 teaspoon

Select loaf size. Have all ingredients at room temperature. Add ingredients to machine according to manufacturer's directions.

Per serving: 91 calories, 3 g protein, 15 g carbohydrate, 2 g total fat (0 g saturated), 14 mg cholesterol, 93 mg sodium, 41 mg potassium.

Basic Easter Bread Dough

1 Pound	Ingredients	1-1/2 Pound
1/2 cup	milk	3/4 cup
1	egg	1
3 tablespoons	margarine *or* butter	1/4 cup
2 cups	all-purpose flour	3 cups
2 tablespoons	sugar	3 tablespoons
1/2 teaspoon	salt	3/4 teaspoon
1 teaspoon	active dry yeast	1 teaspoon

Select dough amount. Add ingredients to machine according to manufacturer's directions. Select dough cycle. When cycle is complete, remove dough from machine. Cover and let rest for 10 minutes. Use the dough in Easter Ring (page 134) or Hot Cross Buns (page 135). (Or, bake the dough in the machine.)

Per serving: 95 calories, 3 g protein, 14 g carbohydrate, 3 g total fat (1 g saturated), 14 mg cholesterol, 101 mg sodium, 37 mg potassium.

EASTER RING

1 Pound	Ingredients	1-1/2 Pound
1 pound recipe	Basic Easter Bread Dough (page 133)	1-1/2 pound recipe
1 tablespoon	margarine *or* butter, melted	2 tablespoons
1/4 cup	packed brown sugar	1/3 cup
1/4 cup	dark raisins	1/3 cup
1/2 teaspoon	ground cinnamon	3/4 teaspoon
1/2 cup	sifted powdered sugar	1/2 cup
1-1/2 teaspoons	water	1-1/2 teaspoons
8	walnut halves	12
8	candied cherries	8
	candied angelica	

Select loaf size. On a lightly floured surface, roll out 1-pound Basic Easter Bread dough to a 16x8-inch rectangle; roll out 1-1/2-pound dough to a 18x10-inch rectangle. Brush with margarine or butter; sprinkle with brown sugar, raisins, and cinnamon. Roll up dough tightly, beginning at a long side; seal by pinching edges together. On a greased baking sheet shape dough into a circle, seam side down. With a sharp knife, make 1/4-inch deep cuts about 1 inch apart on top of the ring just to expose filling. Cover and let rise in a warm place for 30 to 40 minutes or till double.

Bake in a 350° oven for 25 to 30 minutes or till golden brown; cover with foil for the last 10 minutes to prevent overbrowning, if necessary. Cool slightly on a wire rack.

For glaze, stir together powdered sugar and enough water to make of drizzling consistency. Brush ring with glaze while still warm. Garnish with walnuts, cherries, and angelica. Serve warm or cool. Makes 12 or 18 servings.

Per serving: 199 calories, 4 g protein, 33 g carbohydrate, 6 g total fat (1 g saturated), 19 mg cholesterol, 149 mg sodium, 109 mg potassium.

Hot Cross Buns

1 Pound	Ingredients	1-1/2 Pound
1 pound recipe	Basic Easter Bread Dough (page 133)	1-1/2-pound recipe
1/4 teaspoon	ground nutmeg	1/2 teaspoon
1/4 teaspoon	finely shredded lemon peel	1/2 teaspoon
1/3 cup	dark raisins	1/2 cup
1/4 cup	diced candied citron *or* orange peel	1/3 cup
1	beaten egg	1
1 tablespoon	water	1 tablespoon
1/2 cup	sifted powdered sugar	1/2 cup
1 teaspoon	lemon juice	1 teaspoon
1/2 to 1 teaspoon	water	1/2 to 1 teaspoon

Select loaf size. Prepare Basic Easter Bread Dough as directed, except add nutmeg and lemon peel to machine according to manufacturer's dough cycle directions. When cycle is complete, remove dough from machine. Knead in raisins and citron. Cover and let rest for 10 minutes.

Cut 1-pound dough into 12 portions; cut 1-1/2-pound dough into 18 portions. Shape into smooth balls. Place on a greased baking sheet. Cover and let rise about 45 minutes or till nearly double.

If desired, use a sharp knife to score tops of rolls to make a cross. Combine egg and water; brush onto rolls. Bake in a 375° oven for 12 to 15 minutes or till golden brown. Cool slightly on a wire rack.

For icing, stir together powdered sugar, lemon juice, and enough water to make a thick, creamy icing. Make a cross on each bun with the icing. Serve warm or cool. Makes 12 or 18 buns.

Per serving: 178 calories, 4 g protein, 31 g carbohydrate, 4 g total fat (1 g saturated), 36 mg cholesterol, 156 mg sodium, 91 mg potassium.

CHRISTMAS ANISE BREAD

1 Pound	Ingredients	1-1/2 Pound
1/2 cup	milk	3/4 cup
1	egg	1
3 tablespoons	margarine *or* butter	1/4 cup
2-1/4 cups	bread flour	3-1/3 cups
2 tablespoons	sugar	3 tablespoons
1/2 teaspoon	salt	3/4 teaspoon
1/2 teaspoon	aniseed, crushed	3/4 teaspoon
1 teaspoon	active dry yeast	1 teaspoon

Select loaf size. Add ingredients to machine according to manufacturer's directions. Select dough cycle. When cycle is complete, remove dough from machine. Use dough in Jule Kaga (page 137) or Hoska Czechoslavakian Bread (page 138). Or, bake the dough in the machine.

Per serving: 96 calories, 3 g protein, 14 g carbohydrate, 3 g total fat (1 g saturated), 14 mg cholesterol, 100 mg sodium, 38 mg potassium.

JULE KAGA (SWEDISH BREAD)

1 Pound	Ingredients	
1-pound recipe	Christmas Anise Bread (page 136)	1-1/2-pound recipe
1/2 teaspoon	ground cardamom	3/4 teaspoon
1/4 cup	dark raisins	1/3 cup
1/4 cup	sliced candied red cherries	1/3 cup
1/4 cup	diced mixed candied fruits and peels	1/3 cup
1/4 cup	sliced almonds	1/3 cup
1 recipe	Powdered Sugar Icing (page 124)	1 recipe
	sliced candied red cherries	
	sliced almonds	

Select loaf size. Prepare dough for Christmas Anise Bread as directed, except add cardamom to machine according to manufacturer's dough cycle directions. When cycle is complete, remove dough from machine. Knead in raisins, candied cherries, candied fruits and peels, and almonds. Cover and let rest for 10 minutes.

Shape dough into a round loaf. Place on a greased baking sheet. Cover and let rise about 30 minutes or till nearly double. Bake in a 350° oven for 40 to 50 minutes or till golden brown; cover with foil for the last 15 minutes to prevent overbrowning, if necessary. Cool on a wire rack. Frost with Powdered Sugar Icing. Decorate with additional cherries and almonds.

Per serving: 146 calories, 4 g protein, 23 g carbohydrate, 5 g total fat (1 g saturated), 14 mg cholesterol, 126 mg sodium, 88 mg potassium.

Hoska Czechoslavakian Bread

1 Pound	Ingredients	1-1/2 Pound
1-pound recipe	Christmas Anise Bread (page 136)	1-1/2-pound recipe
1/4 cup	dark raisins	1/3 cup
1/3 cup	chopped candied pineapple *or* candied orange peel	1/2 cup
1/3 cup	chopped almonds	1/2 cup
1	beaten egg	1
1 tablespoon	water	1 tablespoon
	sliced almonds	

Select loaf size. Prepare Christmas Anise Bread dough as directed, except add raisins, candied fruit, and almonds to machine according to manufacturer's dough cycle directions. When cycle is complete, remove dough. Cover and let rest for 10 minutes.

Divide dough in half. Separate 1 half of the dough into 3 equal portions. Shape each portion into a 10-inch rope (14-inch ropes for 1-1/2-pound dough). Braid.* Place braid on a large greased baking sheet; brush with water. Divide remaining dough into 4 equal portions. Shape each of 3 of the portions into a 9-inch rope (12-inch ropes for 1-1/2-pound dough). Braid*; place on top of the first braid. Brush with water.

Divide last portion of dough into 2 equal portions. Shape each portion into a 7-inch rope (10-inch ropes for 1-1/2-pound dough). Twist ropes together. Place on top of second braid; press lightly.

Cover and let rise about 45 minutes or till nearly double. Combine egg and water; brush over braid and decorate with sliced almonds, gently pressing them into dough. Bake in a 325° oven for 40 to 45 minutes or till golden. Cool on a wire rack.

*To braid, line up the ropes 1 inch apart. Starting in the middle, loosely bring left rope underneath center rope; lay it down. Then bring the right rope under the new center rope; lay it down. Repeat to end. Then on the other end, braid by bringing the outside ropes alternately over center rope to the center. Press ends together to seal and tuck under.

Per serving: 141 calories, 4 g protein, 20 g carbohydrate, 5 g total fat (1 g saturated), 27 mg cholesterol, 135 mg sodium, 89 mg potassium.

KUGELHOPF

1 Pound	Ingredients
3/4 cup	half-and-half, light cream, *or* milk
1	egg
2 tablespoons	margarine *or* butter
1 tablespoon	brandy
2-1/4 cups	bread flour
2 tablespoons	sugar
1/2 teaspoon	salt
1 teaspoon	active dry yeast
1/4 cup	raisins
1/4 cup	slivered almonds
	powdered sugar

Add the first 8 ingredients to machine according to manufacturer's directions. Select dough cycle. When cycle is complete, remove dough from machine. Knead in raisins and almonds. Cover and let rest for 10 minutes.

Arrange dough in the bottom of a greased 8-1/2-inch diameter Kugelhopf mold or a 5-cup fluted tube mold, stretching dough to fit and pinching ends of dough together.

Cover and let rise about 30 minutes or till nearly double. Bake in a 375° oven for 25 to 30 minutes or till golden brown. Cool in pan on wire rack for 10 minutes; remove from pan and cool completely. Sprinkle with powdered sugar before serving.

Per serving: 120 calories, 4 g protein, 18 g carbohydrate, 3 g total fat (1 g saturated), 14 mg cholesterol, 110 mg sodium, 78 mg potassium.

Basic Danish Bread

1 Pound	Ingredients	1-1/2 Pound
1/2 cup	milk	3/4 cup
1	egg	1
3 tablespoons	margarine *or* butter	4 tablespoons
2 cups	bread flour	3 cups
3 tablespoons	sugar	1/4 cup
3/4 teaspoon	ground cardamom	1-1/4 teaspoons
1/2 teaspoon	salt	3/4 teaspoon
1 teaspoon	active dry yeast	1 teaspoon

Select loaf size. Add ingredients to machine according to manufacturer's dough cycle directions. When cycle is complete, remove dough from machine. Cover and let rest for 10 minutes. Use the dough in Flatbröd (page 141), Mandelbröd (page 142), or Rosinbröd (page 143). Or, bake the dough in the machine.

Per serving: 99 calories, 3 g protein, 15 g carbohydrate, 3 g total fat (1 g saturated), 14 mg cholesterol, 100 mg sodium, 38 mg potassium.

FLATBRÖD (DANISH BRAIDED TWIST)

1 Pound	Ingredients	1-1/2 Pound
1-pound recipe	Basic Danish Bread (page 140)	1-1/2-pound recipe
2 tablespoons	slivered almonds	2 tablespoons
1	slightly beaten egg yolk	1
1 tablespoon	water	1 tablespoon

Select loaf size. Prepare Basic Danish Bread dough as directed, using dough cycle. When cycle is complete, remove dough from machine. Cover and let rest about 10 minutes.

On a lightly floured surface, divide dough into 3 equal portions. Roll each portion into a 12-inch rope (18-inch ropes for 1-1/2-pound dough). To braid, line up the ropes 1 inch apart. Starting in the middle, loosely bring left rope underneath center rope; lay it down. Then bring the right rope under the new center rope; lay it down. Repeat to end. Then on the other end, braid by bringing the outside ropes alternately over center rope to the center. Press ends together to seal and tuck under. Transfer to a greased baking sheet.

Cover and let rise in a warm place about 30 minutes or till nearly double. Combine egg yolk and water; brush onto bread. Sprinkle with almonds.

Bake in a 375° oven for 30 to 35 minutes or till golden brown. Cool on a wire rack. Serve warm or cool.

Per serving: 108 calories, 3 g protein, 15 g carbohydrate, 4 g total fat (1 g saturated), 27 mg cholesterol, 100 mg sodium, 45 mg potassium.

Mandelbröd (Danish Almond Coffeecake)

1 Pound	Ingredients
1-pound recipe	Basic Danish Bread (page 140)
1/3 cup	almond paste
2 tablespoons	margarine *or* butter
1	egg
1/2 cup	sifted powdered sugar
1/4 teaspoon	almond extract
2 to 3 teaspoons	milk

Prepare Basic Danish Bread dough as directed, using dough cycle. When cycle is complete, remove dough from machine. Cover and let rest for 10 minutes.

On a lightly floured surface, roll out dough to an 18x12-inch rectangle. Combine almond paste, margarine or butter, and egg till smooth; spread over dough. Roll up jelly-roll style, starting from one of the long sides, pinch seams to seal. Transfer to a greased baking sheet, curving the loaf into a crescent or horseshoe shape. With scissors, snip roll almost to bottom at 1/2-inch intervals and pull slices alternately to one side, then to the other to show filling. Cover and let rise about 30 minutes or till nearly double.

Bake in a 350° oven about 25 minutes or till golden brown; covering loosely with foil the last 10 minutes to prevent overbrowning, if necessary. Cool slightly on a wire rack.

For icing, in a small bowl combine powdered sugar, almond extract, and enough milk to make an icing of drizzling consistency. Drizzle over loaf and sprinkle with sliced almonds. Serve warm or cool.

Per serving: 148 calories, 34 g protein, 20 g carbohydrate, 6 g total fat (1 g saturated), 27 mg cholesterol, 120 mg sodium, 76 mg potassium.

INDEX

continued on page 144

Better Homes and Gardens®
MORE
BREAD MACHINE
BOUNTY

BETTER HOMES AND GARDENS® BOOKS
Des Moines

BETTER HOMES AND GARDENS® BOOKS

An Imprint of Meredith® Books

President, Book Group: Joseph J. Ward

Vice President and Editorial Director: Elizabeth P. Rice

Executive Editor: Nancy N. Green

Managing Editor: Christopher Cavanaugh

Art Director: Ernest Shelton

Test Kitchen Director: Sharon Stilwell

MORE BREAD MACHINE BOUNTY

Project Manager/Editor: Jennifer Darling

Text and Recipe Writer: Gayle Shockey Hoxter, MPH., R.D.

Graphic Designer: Pam Barton

Test Kitchen Product Supervisor: Jennifer Petersen

Cover Food Stylist: Janet Pittman

Cover Photographer: Mike Dieter

On the cover:

Streusel Kuchen page 130

Herb-Onion Monkey Bread page 58

Wheat, Rosemary, and Tomato Focaccia page 104

St. Lucia Buns page 120

Wheat Cinnamon Rolls page 100

Cornmeal Sourdough Bread page 31

Dill-Onion Wheat Bread page 53

Carrot-Herb Bread page 64

Tomato Bread page 69

Portugese King's Cake page 124

Our seal assures you that every recipe in *More Bread Machine Bounty* has been tested in the Better Homes and Gardens® Test Kitchen. This means that each recipe is practical and reliable, and meets our high standards of taste appeal. We guarantee your satisfaction with this book for as long as you own it.

WE CARE!

We Care! All of us at Better Homes and Gardens® Books are dedicated to providing you with the information and ideas you need to create tasty foods. We welcome your comments and suggestions. Write us at: Better Homes and Gardens® Books, Cookbook Editorial Department, RW-240, 1716 Locust Street, Des Moines, IA 50309-3023

If you would like to order additional copies of any of our books, call 1-800-678-2803 or check with your local bookstore.

MEREDITH® CORPORATION

Corporate Officers: Chairman of Executive Committee: E.T. Meredith III Chairman of the Board, President, and Chief Executive Officer: Jack D. Rehm **Group Presidents:** Joseph J. Ward, Books; William T. Kerr, Magazines; Philip A. Jones, Broadcasting; Allen L. Sabbag, Real Estate **Vice Presidents:** Leo R. Armatis, Corporate Relations; Thomas G. Fisher, General Counsel and Secretary; Larry D. Hartsook, Finance; Michael A. Sell, Treasurer; Kathleen J. Zehr, Controller and Assistant Secretary